PAST LIVES

The Evolution of the Soul

PAUL WILLIAMSON

FIVE KINGS PRESS

An imprint of
Animal Dreaming Publishing

PAST LIVES
The Evolution of the Soul

FIVE KINGS PRESS
An imprint of ANIMAL DREAMING PUBLISHING
PO Box 5203
East Lismore
NSW 2480 Australia

publish@animaldreamingpublishing.com
AnimalDreamingPublishing.com
FiveKingsPress.com
@AnimalDreamingPublishing
@animaldreamingpublishing
@fivekingspress

First published in 2022

ISBN: 978-0-6454206-9-2

The information in this book is intended for spiritual and emotional guidance only. It is not intended to replace medical advice or treatment.

Designed by Animal Dreaming Publishing

Contents

Prelude

The notion of past lives is intriguing. If we have lived other lives besides this one, are we able to remember them? What is it that lies in the depths of our consciousness? Is it safe to go there? Will I find memories from far distant times in history? Are past lives real? What will these 'memories' tell me about my soul? Do I have the courage to explore and delve into these hidden unknown experiences that lure me? If I go there, I may discover things that change me, that give me a different, deeper outlook about my life. Am I prepared to do that? What about my fears? I do not want to find out something that I would not like. Should I listen to my fears? What if it is all stuff that I make up? So many questions. There is much to know.

To learn about our past lives is a spiritual journey of self-discovery. Do we step forward or go another way? It is up to us. The path we tread is our choice.

**

Paul Williamson shares his experiences based on his work as a past life therapist. He has been doing past life regression work professionally for over 33 years.

Acknowledgments

I give thanks to all those teachers who have helped and supported me on my path: those that I have seen, and those who have remained unseen. I express my gratitude to all of you who have opened yourselves to my guidance, doing past life regression with me. It has been a privilege. Finally, I extend my heart-felt appreciation to all the staff at Animal Dreaming Publishing, for your faith in me.

For all you who read this book, may you be blessed on your journey. May the Light of your soul path shine brightly for you, and may your heart be open with love. Thank you.

Introduction

ABOUT PAUL

I was born and brought up with loving, but conventional parents. When I was a child, I was fascinated with the concept of God. My outlook was that at the centre of our existence there was love. I believed that and it was my faith. My parents were Christians, and they took me to church. I was open to faith, prayer, and the need to love one another. Because I sensed that there was a higher loving spiritual power that was with us, I felt protected and hopeful. There were some aspects of the Bible, though, and how it was interpreted that I could not accept. It did not feel right to me that we would only have one life, or that some people would gain exclusive access to Heaven and others would not. It was put to me that the Bible was the source of all truth, but I could not accept that. There had to be something more. I searched for answers, but I did not know where to look. As I grew up, I wondered what would happen when we died. On one side, I was attracted and curious, but I was a little bit afraid and unsure too.

Then, when I was 18, on a Sunday evening, I was listening to various religious broadcasts on the radio, trying to find something which would inspire me. I came across a broadcast by the Theosophical Society. There was a woman speaking about reincarnation and the evolution of the soul. At once, I stopped turning the dial of my radio. I was listening with all my attention — the topics fascinated me. I had to think about what was being said. Over the next months, I made sure that every Sunday, I would listen to these broadcasts. Slowly but surely, I began to accept the teachings that were being spoken. They taught me about a possible spiritual reality that I had not encountered during my upbringing. I found myself resonating with the concept that I could live more than one life, and that each incarnation could help me to grow as a soul. I liked that idea. When I thought about life after death and the notion that I was a wise developing being of Light, that felt true to me too. Life was what I made it to be. All these teachings went deep into my heart. I felt that I had, at last, found a concept and outlook to reality that felt true to me. It felt like I was coming home.

There had to be a continuity of the soul. Our existence was eternal. It had to be like that. If we went through one life to learn lessons and experience what physical life could offer, why not another and another. It made so much sense to me that our soul would advance through lifetimes, and spiritual experiences on Earth. We were responsible for the fulfilment of our own destiny. It all started to connect for me, somehow. When I thought about how life was perpetually changing, it made sense that love and existence was evolving, it was not static. I had so many questions, but so much now felt right, and I felt content with that. Soon I was reading books on the subject and attending talks. My faith in the concept of reincarnation was growing. It was not so much what I read or what anyone said that made the difference. I could feel faith for the reality of reincarnation in my heart. My mind wanted me to test the assumptions I was making but it was important for me to trust what I felt. What if I was wrong?

My thinking doubted, but my heart was sure. I had found a spiritual pathway that had truth. This was my truth, but it might not be the truth for everyone. I began to believe that there could be many pathways to God, and I had to learn more.

Over the next years, I broadened my reading to include books about different religions and spiritual practices around the world. I learnt about reverence, and I gained great respect for people who lived with a sincere spiritual faith. Always, though, I returned to reincarnation as the spiritual teaching that made most sense to me. I could so easily imagine how souls would come to Earth for a physical incarnation and then after their incarnation how they would leave the body and their soul would assimilate the learning from their lived experiences. Then they could plan another life to further their experiences, so that their soul could mature and grow.

It was so easy to imagine this. As a cosmology, it was a view which gave reason for people to be on Earth. If we were souls in a physical body, then our purpose would be to learn inner tasks set by us so that we could progress. It was an engrossing thought. I wanted to find out about my own past lives, and to learn how people could experience them. The Theosophical Society suggested someone must be a very highly evolved soul before they could gain knowledge of past lives. This teaching puzzled me, and I wondered if there was an easier way. The thought of staying in some ashram or cave for fifty years, searching for enlightenment, did not appeal to me. My journey went on.

Some years later, I was living in Scotland at a place called Newbold House, within the Findhorn Foundation, with a New Age spiritual community, and it was like nowhere else I had lived before. From one side of our world to the other,

I had been drawn to it, and it was a place I loved. People believed that we could find God or Spirit by tuning in to our hearts. We were all, in our essence, loving souls, and we had the capacity to live our own sacred journeys. Through meditation and an openness to learn about our deeper selves, we could find our spiritual paths. There were tasks that all of us needed to fulfil in our lives.

Because we were all unique, nobody else could know exactly what our task would be. We had to find out for ourselves. The Findhorn Foundation was a place of hope where people discovered who they were, and while they did so they could live with others in love and harmony. The philosophy of people living in Findhorn was that it was possible for people to achieve peace on Earth. Such thoughts inspired me. This was an environment where I could find kindred spirits from all over the world. My idealism surged with the potentials of what our world could be like.

Where the Theosophical Society had suggested that I could never know about my own past lives because I had to be spiritually advanced, in the environment of Newbold House I felt the strong desire to learn to love and heal others spiritually, not just to be focused upon myself. This, for me, was the beginning. I felt I was being propelled towards a vocation in which I could guide others to awaken to their own spirituality.

As my time at Newbold House continued, I developed leadership skills and began leading personal development residential workshops for people to go on inner journeys to learn about themselves. It was remarkably interesting for me to facilitate processes where people could learn what was deep inside them. People needed to experience their own inner truth. There was so much that could arise through guided meditations and rituals. I wanted to go deeper with people, so they could experience, more fully, the core of their being. Newbold House was a starting point for me, but there reached a point where I felt that I had gone as far as I could go, and I needed something more. I wanted to learn to be a therapist, and then to support people individually.

I left Newbold House and stepped onto a new path. It felt like synchronicity because when I left I also discovered how past life regression therapy using hypnosis was a means through which people could find out about their past lives. I searched through magazines and the directories to find out how I could learn more. At this time there was no internet and hardly any available training of the kind I needed. Finally, I found a course in hypnotherapy that I thought might suit me. Before I could learn about regression, I would have to learn to use hypnosis first.

It was early 1988 when I signed up to do a hypnosis and hypnotherapy course in Scarborough in the UK. My trainer was Wilf Proudfoot who was a brilliant hypnosis practitioner. The training I would receive was quite broad in its scope. Not all the items in the curriculum interested me. However, one of the subjects stood out; included in the course was the study of past life regression. This was the reason I chose to do the training.

The first afternoon my tutor worked with a volunteer to lead him into the memory of one of his past lives is a vivid memory of my own. My eyes were so big with awe as I took in everything that happened. The student seemed to go into quite a deep state and recounted a past life, a simple life in a village some hundreds of years ago. He talked about the stone dwelling he lived in. My tutor asked what the student had been eating and asked many other questions regarding his everyday life. The student was able to answer with his normal voice. At times though, his voice wavered, and he became emotionally affected by his experience. It was as though the memory of the past life was flowing through him. There was one incident he related where he'd become quite sad in his past life. For me, his responses were fascinating. When the tutor ended the regression and the student returned to his normal consciousness, the student seemed quite moved by the experience.

Afterwards, there were animated questions. The experience stimulated an interest in the process for many of us. However, our tutor was less interested. After addressing a few questions, he was ready to move on, and confessed that he did not even believe in past lives. I was disappointed he did not share the same passion in regression that I did. He showed us basic techniques of how it could be done, but only because he regarded it as an interesting phenomenon, not as a meaningful therapy. The presentation from that afternoon was all we did with regression in the whole course.

It was useful for me to learn how easily people could be regressed. But how would I use regression as a personal and spiritual development tool? Perhaps people might find some fascination in learning about their past life identity and accessing some details of their habits? That was what my tutor had focused upon. But how would that help people in their life today? I felt that I still had much to learn.

For the remainder of the training course, there were many other strands of hypnotherapy that were presented but none of them aroused my interest like the regression had. When the training course was completed, I attained my Hypnotherapy Practitioner qualification. But my reason for doing the course had only been partially fulfilled.

The next turning point in my career came when I decided that I would have to teach myself regression. I knew how to administer hypnosis. I would have to experiment to find out more avenues of how the process could work, and how it could be of benefit to people.

I read many books and researched as widely as I could. I asked for volunteers willing to allow me to try regression with them, and there was no shortage! And this is how I began my work with past life regression, by working with friends and family. It was a bit of a trial and error. Some sessions worked better than others. Gradually, I built confidence and found I could trust my intuition about what I needed to do. There was a knowing in me that guided me. The more sessions that I did, the stronger this inner knowing became.

One of my first willing volunteers was my mother. She was curious, and she was interested to help me, however, she was not a believer in reincarnation. When we started the session, I was surprised how easily she went into regression. She went into a past life in Italy. It was very vivid for her, and she still remembers the details of her regression session to this day, and she is now 93 years old.

I felt surges of passion while practicing past life regression. It gave me such joy to be both a facilitator and witness to people connecting with deeply meaningful aspects of who they were. The experiences people had were often quite astounding. I was especially interested in leading people through their past life deaths. My clients would journey to the Light, and this would feel amazing to them. One of my early clients overcame depression after one session where in a past life she was a Native American squaw. Another woman had a growth in her womb which disappeared after she had visited one of her past lives. This was a therapy that was so vibrant and went deeper than any other form of therapy that I had done before.

The more I learnt, the more I wanted to discover. I was a bit like a child in a toy shop. I wanted to explore all aspects of what this therapy could offer. As time went on, I improved and embraced more responsibility. This was not a plaything. I was dealing with people's souls when doing this work. I had to be mindful and compassionate. It was essential that I took proper account of people's wellbeing and needed to ensure that how I facilitated the process would be of value to my clients, as much as was possible.

When I started doing regressions, I was astonished at the variety of experiences that people experienced. However, the basics of what people would experience, like what happened when their soul went through their past life death, all of this was broadly remarkably similar. What I had read about past lives was brought to life in these one-on-one sessions with clients having direct experiences of them. I found people's regression experiences bewilderingly believable, so much so that often even the people were surprised. There was no glorifying of the ego through what was conveyed in the past lives. The tears and emotion, especially the beautiful love people felt in the Spiritual World – all this seemed beyond what people would be able to make up.

My approach to the work was quite different from how my tutor had outlined it in the original training course. What interested me was not about finding out what people had for breakfast in the 1700s, or then determining if the name of the person's past life self could be verified by records. I want-ed to find out how regression could be utilised as a spiritual quest. It did not daunt me that some other mainstream psychotherapists felt strongly that past life experiences should be left alone. To me, past life regression was a fascinating tool for people to learn about who they were, gaining knowledge of their deeper self. And why not? If this could help people to become aware of a deeper sense of meaning of what their lives were truly all about, who they were as a soul, then this had to be a good and incredibly useful inner journey for people to experience.

My commitment to the work grew and I soon felt competent enough to accept paying clients. Opportunities presented to conduct talks, and lead past life workshops. It was all extremely interesting, and it represented a new phase in my life. I had manifested the profession that I wanted to do. At this stage I was living in England with a young family. All was going very well.

DELVING INTO MY OWN PAST LIVES

I was very curious to learn about my own past lives, but how could I do that? I needed to find another person like me. That was not so easy. I met people who claimed to be able to do past life regression, but it wasn't what I was looking for or what I offered. After working with a few people with inconclusive results, I was not sure whether the people who had tried to regress me were lacking in skills as practitioners or whether I was a difficult subject.

Finally, I came across somebody who could help. Her name was Moira. It was rather a fortuitous meeting for she had just moved into the area I lived, exactly at a time I needed to find someone. We got on well and her outlook was like mine. She also regarded regression as spiritual work. Moira was English and had spent some time in Australia, while I was Australian and now spending time in England. Her background was more as a psychic than a therapist, but she seemed to be proficient at therapy, and had learnt regression while she had been in Australia.

When she regressed me for the first time, I felt quite nervous. I did not know if it could work for me, even though I'd seen it work numerous times for others. I was pleased to be able to go into trance quite deeply. For the first few sessions, imagery came to me, but it was vague, and I was not sure if I might be making it all up. I did not want to disappoint Moira because she was good at what she was doing, and I persevered. In the middle of my third regression session with her, after giving some uncertain answers to her questions, I asked Moira for reassurance. Was I getting anything? Moira told me that she could see my past life with her psychic eye, and that what I was telling her was true. I believed her, and as I accepted what she had told me, the imagery, thoughts, and feelings of what I was experiencing began to come to me stronger and clearer. It was like allowing myself to experience a line of another reality which I had not known existed. I just needed to believe that the process could work for me, and then it did.

From my time with Moira, the most interesting past life that came to me was one where I lived in Ancient Greece, about 2,000 BC. It was from a society that existed a long time before Classical Greece. In this life, I was a teacher and healer at the Temple of Delphi. People looked to me for leadership. It was a beautiful, gentle existence where we all lived simply but with a strong spiritual connection. I also had a psychic sense in this life and my third eye was wide open. A group of us from the temple became aware that invaders were coming from far away to the East. We were distraught to realise that these invaders were like an irrepressible force that we could not stop. If they reached our land, they would destroy the temple and our community. I could not accept it and wanted to find a way to prevent them.

We were peace-loving people, but we couldn't let them overrun us. We tried, through collective mind control to put a psychic shield around our existence, to persuade the invaders to go elsewhere. Sadly, we could not tune into their wavelength. Their minds were vastly different to ours, much more brutal and war-like. We were all killed. I was devastated. As I left my body, I felt despair that a community so beautiful and well-meaning could be obliterated in this way.

I realised there were lessons in that life for me about letting go, that I could not control everything. But this life also inspired me. If I had been a healer and teacher then, perhaps I could do something similar in my present life too. It was a past life memory to give me faith in myself.

I was sad when Moira left and returned to Australia after a few months. I missed her support and companionship. However, in the years that followed, there were other people who helped me to access more of my past lives. My strongest inner senses were what I felt and what I knew, whereas when I had been working with others, most people validated their past life experiences through what they saw. It was a great experience for me to uncover knowledge of my past lives, and I felt that I learnt a lot about myself and the journey of my soul. After doing several regressions, I sensed that I had done enough with my own explorations. Now it was time for me to dedicate myself more fully towards helping others so they could make their own discoveries.

FURTHER TRAINING

The training I had received to date still hadn't equipped me with all the skills I felt I needed. How could I support people who went through a big catharsis and became very emotional? What would I do with that? How was the best way for me to help clients to process that emotion? It seemed important to be able to allow the emotion, but I was uncertain how best to help clients channel it.

Strong emotional reactions scared me a little and I did not want my own fears to impinge on my clients' experiences. During regression sessions, strong emotional discharge could occur quite suddenly, and this needed to be released from a client's energy system for them to find peace. I also did not want to suppress my clients' emotional responses because I was uncomfortable dealing with them, so I had to learn how to manage this aspect of past life processing productively.

In the early 1990s, I became aware of the teachings of Dr Roger Woolger. He had written a book on past life therapy, called *Other Lives, Other Selves*. After I attended some of Dr Woolger's talks and workshops, I enrolled in a three-year past life therapy training course with Dr Woolger. He was a trauma release expert and a trained Jungian analyst.

One of my first memories of him, was when he gave a demonstration of regression in front of a hundred people or so in Manchester, England. He used techniques that could quickly guide people into deep states of consciousness without hypnosis, where they would access past life memories and release copious amounts of emotion, all within minutes of him starting the process. After he had finished his work, the volunteers would emerge from their regressions smiling. The methods he used were incredible.

Doing his training workshops was certainly a recipe for me to overcome my discomfort with the therapeutic expression of emotions. He would guide us into group regressions paired up with another trainee facilitator. From one end of the room to the other, there would be screams, bellows of rage, convulsions of tears and the shaking of fears being released. There was no suppression of emotional expression here. I loved it, and I learned such a lot about how to deal with emotional release.

To witness someone going through an intensely emotional releasing session and then coming out of it feeling relieved and at ease gave me heart and confidence. This training gave me the tools I was seeking so that I could help people in the way I felt I needed to.

CHANNELLING

Before I started training with Dr Woolger, I had been working with a woman called Marjorie Wilson and her husband Reg. Through Marjorie, I learnt about the existence of Spirit Guides. Prior to meeting Marjorie, I had been very sceptical about the reality of Spirit Guides. I had come across many people claiming to have some fanciful Spirit Guides from some extraterrestrial origins. These people did not impress me. It seemed to be just a glamour trip, which people used to enhance their spiritual standing. However, meeting Marjorie changed that.

Marjorie was one of the humblest people I could have met. She was a woman in her late 50s who was crippled with painful rheumatoid arthritis. Doing regression, for her, was both an inner comfort and an interest. Marjorie enjoyed being occupied in her inner worlds and doing sessions with me, where she learnt more about herself. During one session, Marjorie ventured into the Spiritual World. I asked if anyone there could help her. Her wondrous and eloquent Spirit Guide Sojah presented. Marjorie felt so moved by the spiritual love that she felt emanating from Sojah, it was almost overwhelming.

Needing to validate this in myself, I asked myself this question: Was Sojah an actual spiritual entity with independent existence, or was he some creation of Marjorie's inner consciousness? I considered this in different ways. One factor that helped convince me that Sojah was a spiritual entity was the degree to which Marjorie became very emotional when she was in Sojah's company, evident in her facial expressions and her bodily reactions. She could feel his love strongly, and what he conveyed to her through his thoughts helped her greatly. There was no hint of self-aggrandisement through the process. When Marjorie channelled Sojah, her head would go down and then, when Marjorie was in deep trance, her head would rise slowly, and her speaking voice would be quite different and hold a dignity and self-assurance that was vastly different to how Marjorie normally expressed herself. It was enough, cumulatively over time, to convince me.

I began to be open to the existence of Spirit Guides. I work-ed more with Marjorie and Sojah and listened to Sojah's teachings about Spirit Guides. He channelled through Marjorie, imparting information about how all of us had loving Spirit Guides and he taught us of their purpose. After we left an incarnation on Earth, our Spirit Guide would be there to comfort us and to help us come to terms with the life that we had lived. Our Guide was a Higher Being who was further along their path than us, a very loving and perceptive being who generally would know us better than we knew ourselves. I felt that enabling people to connect with their Spirit Guides was another worthwhile tool and resource that I could introduce to my clients.

After 18 months of inner explorations, Marjorie, Reg, and I started a public healing group; a group that continued for over ten years. I learnt so much about the Spiritual World through this group. It also became important for me to learn about my own Spirit Guide. Sometimes I had meditations where I could sense quiet thoughts coming into my mind. These thoughts had a quality of peace to them that was so much quieter than any thoughts that I would generate myself. During one episode of emotional turmoil, I reached my arms upward and asked my Guide to help me. Immediately, I felt a rush of energy cascading through my body. This energy gave me so much serenity; all the turmoil was suddenly gone. I was able to work out what I needed to do then, and all was well. This must have been my Guide – what else could it have been?

I came to believe in the existence of wise Spirit teachers and Angels who could connect with us from the Spiritual World. These beings are important components of our spiritual existence. The teachings from Sojah indicated that our Spirit Guides travelled with us, protecting our space, while we are incarnated on Earth. We are not left here alone. Even if our inner perception is not open, we still have access and all we needed to do was to call and our Guides will approach.

As part of my work with Marjorie and Sojah, I created meditations to help people to connect with their Spirit Guides. It seemed that when people died at the end of a past life and ascended to the Spiritual World, their Spirit Guide would be present to help them learn, as a soul what this lifetime had been about. The Guide would be like a spiritual counsellor, helping a person to find perspective and understanding. I felt immensely grateful to Marjorie and Sojah for all the spiritual awareness that I gained through their help.

LIFE BETWEEN LIVES® THERAPY

In the early 1990s while I was training with Dr Roger Woolger, I became aware of the book *Journey of Souls* written by Dr Michael Newton. My intuition told me that someday I would learn much more about the work of this man. Dr Newton had worked with thousands of clients to enable them to open their awareness to who they were as a soul in the Spiritual World. He would guide his clients to explore higher dimensions of reality. He called this exploration Life Between Lives® Therapy. The accounts which his clients recalled gave them tremendous insights about the nature of their essence. They also learnt about their soul purpose in their life today.

The accounts he gave were fascinating. They gave much personal insight and understanding about the nature of the Spiritual World, and how we, as souls, expressed ourselves in these realms.

It was about 18 years later when I finally trained in the work that Dr Newton did. I joined a training course and became a Life Between Lives® Practitioner with the Newton Institute. The course was remarkably interesting and comprehensive. I learnt many new skills and opened further the scope of what I could offer.

It was important for people to experience the Spiritual Worlds when they left their past life body and died. It was a marvellous healing experience to channel their souls, and so helpful to be able to put that past life behind them. From my work with Dr Roger Woolger, I had gained knowledge of how much psychotherapy it was possible to accomplish in the Spiritual Worlds. Here souls could meet other souls, and complete unresolved communication, unfold to fuller perspectives and open to insights and spiritual understanding. This was all incredibly powerful and healing work. However, what I learned through the Newton Institute was about the potential that existed for people to channel the direct experience of being in the Spiritual Worlds where their soul lived.

I had my own experience of Life Between Lives® Therapy during my training. When I was in the Spiritual World, I felt such a lot of peace. My perception told me that my home on Earth was not just one place, but that the whole Earth was my home. After my session, it was as if I was more certain in my actions. I knew what was important for me to do. Within me, I was more aligned to my soul. I began to travel and explore more of our beautiful world. I could not be content anymore with staying in one place.

Over the years, I have learnt enormously, not only through the trainings that I have had, but also through the thousands of clients who have worked with me. Each client I have worked with has given me their trust. Each of us has a unique soul that is sacred and precious, and I have felt privileged to witness people's souls through the work that I have done. To help people awaken to their souls has been wonderful to facilitate and observe. It has been my duty of care to do my best to treat each client with the utmost respect.

These have been some of my personal experiences. Now I need to share what I know about the subject of past lives so you can learn more about you.

INTRODUCING PAST LIFE REGRESSION

LIVING OTHER LIVES

The concept of past lives connects with the theory of reincarnation, suggesting we do not just live one lifetime, but that we can have many incarnations on Earth. Each lifetime builds upon the others that we have experienced and contributes to our personal evolution. The eternal individual consciousness that we have is called the soul. In between physical lifetimes our soul resides in a loving Spiritual World, which is our spiritual home. We all have a unique history as a soul. If we are quite a young soul, then we may have had only a small number of physical incarnations. Souls who are more mature, may have had many, many lifetimes, not just on Earth but perhaps on other worlds as well.

In each human lifetime, aspects of our soul combine with the foetus while it is in the womb. That combination of elements forms our human self. It is our soul that gives our human self its consciousness, and our soul stays in that physical body for however long that body lives. When the body dies, the physical remains and the spiritual forces within those remains return to the Earth. Meanwhile, the soul leaves the body and ascends to the Light of the Spiritual World where the soul assimilates all the inner learning from that lifetime.

Past lives are lives that we have already lived. The memory of them is in some historical period where we have had a body, either male or female. The lifetime is different to the life that we are living now, but for our soul it connects to our life today, somehow. Every life has learning for the soul to accomplish, and that learning has continuation. If we stay true to our path, we gain maturity as souls by achieving what we set out to do during our various physical incarnations, and by what we learn in the Spiritual World. If we make mistakes by allowing our freewill to lead us in directions away from what our soul intended, then we do not learn those soul lessons. We may need to repeat those lessons for ourselves in another lifetime.

EXPERIENCING PAST LIFE REGRESSION

Past life regression is an intentional experience that allows us to access memories of our past lives that exist in our consciousness. We might have felt moments of déjà vu where people or places seem familiar to us inexplicably. In our dreams, we could have had experiences of ourselves as a different personality in another lifetime. In our dream state, these experiences may seem very real, and we will probably wonder where they come from. There may be flashes of memory that come into our minds that seem to be from other lifetimes. These can spontaneously reveal themselves to our consciousness, without any warning. All these experiences are suggestive of reincarnation. When we engage in past life regression, this brings to the surface of our inner awareness experiences that are already there.

When people initially access the memory of one of their past lives, some adjustment of consciousness is needed. Typically, people may only be aware of some details at first, but with questioning more aspects of the experience reveal themselves. For instance, someone may be aware of standing next to a tree. In the beginning, that may be all that they perceive. But then, with questioning, their consciousness starts to open. More details of the tree and surrounding countryside may become apparent. The person may then become aware of the ground under their feet and the clothes they are wearing. The therapist can ask open questions to stimulate a response from the person's inner consciousness. Once the person can keep their focus on what they inwardly perceive, more of the memory can emerge. Gradually, impressions of memories from the past life reveal themselves more and more.

The therapist can ask their client whether they are male or female. They could answer easily, but sometimes there is an extended silence. If the person realises that in their past life that they are the opposite sex to who they are now, then this can be an unexpected revelation. As the person accepts this, it takes them deeper into the experience. Knowing whether a person was male or female will allow more of the past life experience to emerge.

Often, when people first start to recall their past life, it is as a still image. At some point though, the experience starts to move and become more alive. The person then feels as if they are present in the memory of the past life. It can feel like it is happening now. When in regression, a person becomes increasingly aware, not only of what is happening, but of the thoughts, feelings, and body sensations of their past life self. It will feel as though this person is you.

For me as a therapist, it is helpful when people begin to perceive their past life coming to life. Then it is possible through questioning to suggest that they can experience earlier and later events from the past life. From the past lifetime that the person accesses, it is possible for them to experience memories from the time of birth or before, right through all moments of that life till they die, and even beyond that.

The memory of the past life will be set in some historical period where lifestyle and ways of being could be vastly different from what we know today. Our present-day mind will try to interpret the experiences which are revealed, but we may be likely to struggle to understand all that is there. For instance, there may be cooking utensils or dwelling places that are made of materials unfamiliar to us. Our past life self may have strong feelings for another person that is with them. We could feel those emotions before we understand who that other person is, or the nature of the relationship. It will be like a tapestry that discloses its story and meaning to us, thread by thread.

To prepare for the past life memory to come forth, a person is first guided into a passive state of relaxation by the therapist. This is an induction process that helps them be receptive. Some people take a long time to relax while others relax quite quickly. Once in this relaxed state, it is possible for a person to channel the experience of the past life from within their own consciousness. What is accessed from the past life memory is likely to be as much a surprise to the therapist as it is to the person.

In response to the therapist's questions during regression, suddenly there may be a whole new vista of memory perceptions that open up. Even if the therapist asks a leading question, such as: 'Are you wearing green clothing?' the person is unlikely to see they are suddenly wearing something green. They are more likely to tell the therapist what clothing they are wearing rather than conjuring an outfit that is coloured green. It is not recommended for therapists to ask leading questions though. When I am working with my clients, I remain as neutral as possible, acting as an interested questioning self, rather than being someone who knows what is in the past life. When experiencing regression, a person needs to feel as free as possible to let the regression express itself. A clear experience of the past life comes to the person most easily when the therapist is steady, emotionally supportive and asking open questions.

As the memory of the past life emerges, so will the story of it. There could be peaks and troughs, just as any life has. The most fascinating moment for many is the experience of death. It may have been a peaceful or violent death, or something in between. The moments before the death may be of high anxiety, regret or calm anticipation. From the moment of the last breath, you will experience yourself rising out of the body. This may occur suddenly or gradually. Perhaps you may not want to leave. However it happens, as soon as you are free from that body, you feel an immediate change of state. Usually, people feel peaceful and glad to be out of the restriction of the physical body. Accompanying this is a sense of growing calmness and personal autonomy. Often people feel exhilaration to be flying through space. Sometimes people linger in an in between state, but sooner or later, rise to the Light.

This transition is a universal experience that happens to everyone going through regression to a past life. It will make you wonder if you can expect something similar when you leave your present-life body at the end of your life this time.

Past life regression is a direct living experience that emerges from your inner consciousness. Even for people who do not believe in past lives, they can still inadvertently find themselves experiencing another lifetime that impresses itself upon their awareness.

Most people seem to carry the memories of past lives, but not everyone. I have worked with people who, in all other ways, are good hypnotic subjects, but when I have asked their consciousness to reveal a past life, it has not been there. Perhaps they have experienced light, other colours, or a feeling of love, but there has been no past life. In these cases, I have usually checked and challenged these responses, with no change to the result. Such people often know that they have no past lives and are not surprised by the outcome. They are probably souls having their first life on Earth. I remember one woman who felt very happy when she discovered this. It was joyful for her that she had so much potential in front of her.

Past life regression is generally a very pleasant, relaxing experience. If there are upsetting moments in the past life, you will feel the fear, or trauma, but you will know that this is from your past life, not from your life now You can let the experience flow through you and release it.

When a client comes to a past life therapy session with a fixed idea of what they will access from their past lives, then the process is likely not to work so well for them. It is their ego that has the idea of what they want to experience. The ego wants to dictate what happens and how it all turns out and will block the inspiration of the memories from their inner consciousness from revealing themselves. Past life memories only present themselves when you are open, when you are ready to surrender to whatever may be there. If you try to control what comes forward, you will block it.

The past life that emerges from within you will occur spontaneously, and it is likely to astonish you with its content. It is necessary for you to trust in the process. This is not always easy for people to do. However, by relaxing and just taking things one step at a time, you are likely to feel quite astounded when the impressions start to come through. Then, as the experience proceeds, you may feel even more amazed.

COMING TO TERMS WITH THE REGRESSION EXPERIENCE

When we have been through a past life regression, it is natural to question it. There might have been some moments when we were not quite sure of what was happening, when we seemed to lose it. Some imagery may remind us of a film that we have seen, and we may wonder if our subconscious mind has latched onto that and built a story around it. Perhaps we did not see very much of what was going on, but we had to rely on our feelings. How much do we believe?

How do we trust that the regression memories are authentic? How can we reconcile our past experiences with our normal conscious self? What if there was more to the past life than what we accessed? There could be a lot of questions. As we contemplate further, more thoughts may arise, and more answers may give us further knowledge of what happened in the past life. It is natural that we want to make sense of it all.

For a while, it may occupy us a lot. The feelings in it could have felt very real in places. Then, we might find ourselves feeling very emotional about some of the things that occurred. Some of what we perceived might have touched us deeply. We may want to dismiss these feelings because we are way out of our comfort zone. We are not able to do that easily because what we have experienced will be a challenge to how we regard our reality. There will be a new perception of reality, presenting itself from deep inside us.

For us to access the past life, we will have had to surrender to it. Part of us may have wanted to pull back during the experience, but if we had we would have stopped the experience from flowing. The curiosity in us will always want to know more, but the fearful part may want to shut it down.

Another aspect of the regression is that it is likely to have helped us to learn more about our self and our own psychology. It is an aspect of our inner consciousness expressing itself. When we start to contemplate on it, and more details reveal themselves to us, we may discover that there was more depth of meaning in what was being expressed than we realised. Most likely, we have gained insights from the past life that resonates with how we experience our life today.

A person may also be interested about the historical period of their past life and research the details. They might reflect how when the past life body died, that they were suddenly experiencing themself out of that body, feeling suddenly free and light, released from that body. They could be ascending through the clouds, into space and then into an intense Light. Other beings may be present as well, Light Beings. This would have been vastly different from being on Earth. It would have felt like it was in another dimension of consciousness. When in the Spiritual World, a person is not channelling an experience of being in a body on Earth anymore.

It might be hard to dismiss the Spiritual World experience, for when visited it will feel familiar and like an authentic memory. It feels like home, more homelike than being on Earth. A person may even meet loved ones in Spirit. If they did, they would feel the closeness of being with them. However, it is a different love from what was felt on Earth. There is less attachment and a greater sense of understanding and appreciation. Love extends outwards from you to all beings that are there, and it feels joyous. It is like a universal love, so different but so natural too.

If you did meet the soul of someone you had known on Earth, someone who had passed, then they may have seemed different, younger perhaps, but they would likely have been welcoming. Meeting them in the Spiritual World may have helped you have faith that the Spiritual World does exist and bring you peace.

At the end of a session when you return to your normal consciousness you may struggle to open your eyes. Perhaps you were not even aware of your body while you were experiencing the past life. You could be a bit lightheaded and need some help from your therapist to bring you fully into your body and to be grounded. It is as through you were experiencing the memories using your energetic body rather than your physical body, which may have been the case. Your energy body could have detached itself from your physical body during the regression, so you were able to immerse yourself in the experience of the past life more fully. You may not even have been aware of what was going on around you in our normal reality while you were going through the past life.

When our energetic body can detach from our physical self somewhat, it has more freedom to connect with past life and in between lives memory and awareness. In our normal consciousness, our energy body functions within our physical body, but it can loosen itself from us to go into these experiences.

This is something that we would need to come to terms with too. The regression experience suggests that our physical body is just a vessel for our energy body and soul to inhabit. It could be that we are not merely a physical body with skin and bones and all the physical matter that contributes to our identity. Our body is like a window into the three-dimensional world that we know, while our soul consciousness opens to other dimensions.

There will be much for you to integrate and accept after having your regression session.

WHAT ROLE DOES THE IMAGINATION PLAY IN PAST LIFE REGRESSION?

Our imaginations are remarkable faculties within our minds. Imagination generates our creative ability and is the vehicle for us to be inspired. It enables us to inwardly conceive images or mental constructs with our senses that we may have never fully perceived before. We may dismiss our imagination because it does not operate based on rational thought. The basis upon which we imagine things is not always true.

For instance, we might hear a noise outside our house, and from that noise we may build from our imagination and expectation the fear that there is an intruder. The more we consider this possibility, the more we may start to build a threatening scenario within our minds and be ready to defend ourselves. Our imagination stimulates our emotional response. In fact, the noise may be a branch that has fallen from a tree and not an intruder at all. The creative power of our imagination will have brought into being an inner reality that was a fantasy, and our feelings and nervous system would have been affected by the thoughts and images in our minds.

There are other ways imagination can be expressed. Consider the brilliant mind of the composer, Mozart. On many occasions he would suddenly find that in his inspired imagination there would a complete original symphony from beginning to end. It was not so much that he had created it, but more that the symphony was already there. He had perhaps called for it, and his inner consciousness had responded, and the symphony revealed itself. Mozart was therefore the channel through which this symphony could be composed. From allowing the conception of the symphony to be in his inner mind, all he had to do was to notate it. Then it was grounded as a piece of music that musicians could perform.

Imagination acted as a channel for some inspired vibrational energy of tones and music that could be relayed to Mozart. He was sensitive enough and committed to receive it and to bring it to full expression. Not all of us are quite at the genius level of Mozart, but you may recognise this creative process as being like one you go through in allowing some inspired idea or thought to come to you. With this supposition, the imagination can be a channel for us to connect with higher vibrations and energy that wants to be given to us.

Apparently, Einstein used to conceive through his imagination sublime truths about the nature of our universe. Then he would work with mathematics to try to find the formula that will fit what his intuition and imagination was informing him to be true. In his case, it was not his dynamic rational thought processes that gave him the answers for his profound discoveries about matter and energy. He gained his perception of truth through a process of revelation through his imagination.

There are at least two ways in which our imagination is utilised. One way is when our desires, fears and freewill become involved and what is generated is fantasy; the other way is where the imagination acts as a channel to higher realities to bring forth experiences that are deeply meaningful and with truth.

How does past life regression fit into this? When we

invoke past life regression experiences, we are utilising our imagination as a channel whereby we bring forth experiences and memory that originate from beyond our normal present-day self. The experience of the memory is revealed to us. Used in this way, we can use discipline for our imagination as a spiritual practice and honour our imagination as a faculty within us which can channel truth. Our imagination can become a tool for inner contemplation and connection with the Divine. When we utilise our imagination in this way, we can access past lives, and open our spiritual awareness.

The sceptical part of our mind is called our ego. Our ego tends to be narrow in its outlook. It tends to dismiss our imagination as being the bearer of meaningless fantasy and it will shut down beliefs that suggest we can use our imagination more productively. If we do not believe that we can channel any form of truth through our imagination, then we are not open to it. What we do not believe does not exist. It can very much limit us if we allow our ego to control what we do.

The potential is there if we allow ourselves to believe in the power of the imagination as a vehicle of truth, and if we are open to consider the truth of what we channel. If we have strong spiritual faith, then our openness will be even greater. We can encourage our imagination to reveal fascinating and enthralling experiences and allow our imagination to serve us much better by honouring it rather than being excessively critical of it. Using our imagination as a receptacle to channel experiences does not tell us whether past lives are true or not. However, by accepting the transcendent capacity of our imagination, it does open the gateway so that we can explore what exists within us.

DIFFERENT WAYS TO ACCESS PAST LIVES

The following methods of how people access past life memories are not exclusive, and many people can access through more than one of these means. It certainly makes the process easier for me as a therapist when this is the case. Mostly, though, I find that people have a leading inner sense. This could be 'seeing', 'feeling', 'knowing' or 'body awareness'. It is likely that one of those approaches comes to you more naturally than the others. However, people also benefit when they can be adaptable and are able to respond to a variety of approaches.

VISUAL

If you are someone who has a strong visual capacity, when you access one of your past lives you will see details of the surroundings of where you live. Some people can visualise very clearly, and all the details of scenes will be as clear as they can see now. The images may be a continuous stream of events like watching a movie, or there could be flashes of images. You could be like an observer, watching the drama that is going on rather than being directly involved. If you are watching the experience as an observer, in one of my sessions I would encourage you to be in the body of the person so you can experience the memory of the past life much more fully. This allows you to identify with and experience things through the eyes of your past life self, and connects you with their feelings, thoughts, and energy as if these things are yours.

As humans we tend to rely on our sight to confirm validity of what is going on around us. Our critical self may need to be convinced that we are experiencing something unusual to be willing to proceed. But not everyone has a capacity to see visions when they are doing regression. Some people do not see images internally. However, there are different ways of perceiving besides being visual. You may instead process through your feelings.

FEELING

If you are a feeling type, it may take a while to learn how to use feelings as the primary means of accessing past lives. You might feel the temperature of the air or know whether your clothes are comfortable. If you have spatial awareness, you may perceive whether you are in a confined space or out in the open, or any other dimensions of your experience. As a feeling type, when you begin to connect with a past life self, you will sense their feelings and emotions.

The kind of emotional reactions that our past life self has can deepen our feeling of connection. This can be quite settling for the regression, but also unnerving when the emotional responses are intense. As a feeling type, it can be quite confronting when you experience a sudden burst of emotion in a regression. Sometimes your body may go through some strong emotional release without us even knowing consciously what it is about.

There is a process for managing such an outpouring of emotions. By breathing into the emotions that express themselves, we find awareness of what has been precipitating the release of feelings, and the memory will reveal itself. When we have a visual capacity then the perception of what is happening in the past life is immediate, but we may not have the depth of connection with the past life unless we are feeling it. When the past life memory is coming to us as feeling impressions, then our perception of what is taking place grows and forms itself more gradually than through visual recognition. The outpouring of emotions can be immediate, but our understanding of what it is about will take longer to form. Once we do understand, though, it will be a deep comprehension.

After a public talk about past life regression in Scotland, I asked for a volunteer to have a short sample regression session so I could demonstrate the beginnings of the regression process. I guided this woman into a relaxed state. However, when I got to the point where I would ask my volunteer about her past life, she said that she could see nothing. When I asked again, she repeated that there was nothing there, and that it was all dark. I began to feel somewhat embarrassed and nervous that I may not have chosen an easy subject. Gently, I asked my volunteer to continue to breathe into what she was experiencing. She took some deep breaths, then told me that she still could not see anything–but her feet were cold. I encouraged my volunteer to breathe into the feeling of what she was experiencing. Then she told me that she was standing in snow. Soon, she was able to enlarge upon this, and using her feeling and knowing sense, she was able to give details of the environment where she was, and the clothes that she was wearing.

My volunteer was someone who had a strongly developed feeling inner sense, but her visual capacity was limited. I was happy and relieved when my volunteer began to describe her past life, and she described it from a feeling perspective. It formed a good teaching point for me to tell everyone about the way she accessed her past life memory.

KNOWING

We can also approach our perception purely through knowing. This means of accessing our past lives is through use of our intuition. To use this method, we need to allow a stream of consciousness to flow through us. Thoughts and a sense of knowing come to us and we instinctively know that these perceptions are from a deeper place than our usual thought patterns. For this to work, we need to trust in the stream of consciousness that presents itself, and then involve ourselves in that. We are not able to anticipate the flow of this beforehand.

When we rely upon our inner knowing as the leading source of channelling our past life memory, there may be fleeting images and instances of feeling. These add to our validation of the process. Some of us may find that using our knowing as our means of channelling those past life memories is the most effective and reliable way that we can do it. This is a process that can be learnt. It is a dream-like state where our mental faculties are expressing themselves most strongly.

When I first began to access my past lives, I used this technique. As I grew to believe in the power of my mind and inner consciousness to deliver the memory of my past life to my awareness, it worked very well. At times, I would have to concentrate and give the stream of consciousness that was emerging, my detailed attention. It would be like burrowing into my consciousness, and as I did so, I could sense my inner mind opening. I had to trust that what came to me was true. The thoughts and knowing from the experience would be unlike anything that I had previously imagined or anticipated.

BODY INTELLIGENCE

Another approach that works with some people is working with body intelligence and energies. When the memory of a past life is invoked, we feel sensations in our body. Our body might want to move in response to the memories, and it could occur in quite unpredictable ways. It may be in the way of energetic reactions, including tensions and releasing. This method can be particularly applicable to the releasing of trauma from past lives. Our consciousness might not want us to see the details of the trauma, but our body awareness connects with the memory. Our body could shake or shudder, sometimes uncontrollably. Rather than trying to stop it, we need to surrender to this process. There could be emotions associated with this, or words. As we let all this out from within us, we also release energy conglomerates from the past that we no longer need. Our body has its own self-healing mechanism. When we let our body move naturally with the flow of our inner consciousness, then much very deep healing can be done.

I once worked with a man whose body became very contorted during his sessions. He was not somebody who responded to more conventional inductions to past life memory. For him, his body could express the past life memory, and that was the only way that he could do it. When he went into the memory, he made sounds of suffering, and his body writhed around. It seemed both to him and me that he was reliving experiences of sexual abuse and releasing the pain of it. After a few sessions, the reactions in his body became less pronounced and the intensity of what he experienced lessened. He had been a person carrying a lot of tension in his body. As he continued with the sessions, his body was experiencing much more peace. In his final session, his body was moving around again, and it seemed that his body energy was accessing a sexual experience, but this one was a positive experience, one that he was able, for the first time, to enjoy. The healing was tremendous for him. As he left me at the conclusion of that session, he was smiling and happy. His therapy worked with me, and his process was complete.

The only problem working with body intelligence, is that it is not always so easy to obtain specific information about where the life was taking place, and other quantitative details. This is because the accessing of the memory is through energetics rather than mental recall.

QUESTIONS PEOPLE ASK

MOST ASKED QUESTIONS

I have practised past life regression in Australia and the UK for over 33 years. During that time, I have worked with thousands of people who have gone through a huge variety of past life experiences. Whether or not you have had a past life regression, the following section may provide some answers for you. These are a selection of my most asked questions.

Can we prove that past lives exist?

While it is difficult to gain absolute proof of the existence of past lives, there are still many indications that past lives do exist. For instance, when people access their memories of past lives through regression, they may be aware of their past life name, home address and town, important dates and events from the period, and many other details that can be factually verified. Many of my clients have researched aspects of their regression and consulted historical records and archaeological findings. What they generally find is that their experiences correlate very closely with known sources of history. Very often what they discover is startling to them. These kinds of connections can be very convincing.

However, sceptics can doubt this and speculate whether the information for the past life has come from something the person has read or seen on a film. It is a fact that the mind can contrive a story to fit in with whatever was already known from some subliminal source, but this doesn't factor in how a regression experience can feel very real and personal to the person experiencing it as well as the therapist. It can be countered that if someone was subconsciously contriving a regression memory, then there would be discrepancies and a lack of coherence. In fact, although regression recall can be complex, subtle, and encompassing many varied situations, the threads of what the lifetime presents tend to be remarkably consistent and believable in their context.

Sceptics also put forward the argument that what the subject is accessing comes from genetic memory rather than any genuine experience of another lifetime. Although I have come across some examples of where people appear to have accessed the lifetime of one of their ancestors, I have found this to be quite rare. If genetic memory were the prevailing means by which people accessed their past lives, I would expect that the indications of this happening would be much more widespread, but this is not the case. Rather, people often regress to past lifetimes where the identity of the person they were in their past life has an altogether different genetic signature than any that would fit with their genetic background.

Another dismissive argument about past life regression, suggests that when people are in a form of hypnotic trance, they are picking up the memory imprints or imported memories of some other soul or entity who may have lived a life on Earth previously. The argument is that the past life memories are not actual memories at all and are some form of delusion.

However, the people accessing a past life feel the identity of the person in the past life to be their own identity. It is an experience that is strange, but also quite familiar. There is understanding and insight within the past life that resonates with their life today. They may even identify other souls from the past life as being the same souls that they know today. When those other people correlate this connection through their own past life memory, this is very convincing evidence to suggest that the memory of the past life is what it appears to be.

What happens when we die in our past life?

The lead up to death in a past life regression is as varied as deaths are. For some, the moments before death can be very peaceful with a gradual drifting away, and others, the experience of dying can be abrupt, and even shocking and unexpected. In the latter cases, strong emotions can be engendered. If a person dies in an accident or through an act of violence, death may be so sudden that there is no preparation. A death through suicide involves a wilful decision to end life and can elicit many conflicting emotions.

Whatever the moments are leading up to our death, once the body dies the soul leaves the body. In regression, we experience ourselves apart from the body. We may move rapidly away or linger close by. We might feel relief, or perhaps we may not have wanted to leave loved ones behind. We could feel confused: we may want to comfort our loved ones, but we cannot reach them physically.

As we process this transition, we feel peace and freedom. This peace enables us to feel assured. For most of us, we accept what has happened and are ready to go home. That journey inevitably leads us upwards.

For others, there may be issues to be resolved before making that step. Our path is to go home to the Spiritual World, but some may not want to face it. They could be ashamed and guilty about what was done in this life. It is possible they could feel angry with God or the Divine Source. They may blame those Higher Powers for what has happened during their lives. Another reaction could be not to accept passing over and feel rebellious about moving on. Such souls could then become earthbound spirits and create their own illusory worlds rather than move on. There are also souls who are determined to wait for a loved one before they go anywhere.

We have freewill, even after we leave our physical body. The process of what we do is up to us. The natural route is for us to go upwards and return to what we know is home. It is like a magnetic pull that draws us to go there. If we are in a quandary, we can always ask for inner help. Other Spirit Beings respond when we seek support.

Once we make the step and journey towards the Spiritual World, we feel freedom to be ourselves. Any restriction that we felt in life on a physical level goes. Gradually, we untangle ourselves from emotional and mental restrictions. As we go higher, there is Light, often a brilliant Light and other souls will be waiting to meet us. Here, our heart opens, and we can heal and relax deeply.

The life review is often done after we have adjusted to being a soul in the Spiritual World again. Then we will have the perspective to consider what the life was truly all about. Often, we will need higher beings to point out aspects of the learning in that lifetime that we may have overlooked.

The scope and perspective of the Spiritual World is enormous compared to what we can appreciate in our physical bodies. The change might be an adjustment through stages, or it might be immediate. There may be special places we need to go here, and as we journey these places feel familiar to our soul, but for our present-day self these spiritual places could be astonishing.

The experience of channelling our past life self as it goes into the Spiritual World opens our inner perception tremendously. We embrace the soul consciousness of who we really are, and this can be quite revolutionary. At the same time, we feel joyful recognition to be in this realm again. We reacquaint ourselves with our Higher Self. We can feel a great sense of beauty and wonder in the Spiritual World.

What we experience of it, though, depends on how open we are inwardly and how willing we are to stretch our usual human perception into the unknown.

How do I cope with being in a difficult or challenging position in a past life?

Sometimes people fear that they will not like the past life that they access. When they confront themselves in a past life that appears distasteful, they may feel some uneasiness and therefore will not want to approach it in case it will upset them. There may be some basis to these instinctive reactions, and this will be a test for the person as to whether they are willing to go through it or not.

We cannot control what lifetime comes forward for us. Our inner consciousness does not necessarily choose the past life that is most comfortable. The soul selects that lifetime which would be most needed for our inner growth, and therefore such experiences can be challenging for us. We do not grow when things are too easy, and we learn most when confronting weaknesses and finding ways to be stronger. The past life could well be one to help us grow and be stronger so it may be a difficult one, and not one where we were at our best.

From tough lives, we can learn from our mistakes. Whatever we did wrong in that past life, or whatever our limitations were then, they are from the past, and we can do better now. We do not have to be attached to what happened in that past life, because it is over. It is about what we can learn from our past endeavours. It is our ego which is fanciful and wants us to be in a good and glorious light. This is not how things happen. Each life has its learning, and how can you learn if you do things perfectly, if there are no painful dilemma that you must confront?

Our souls, in each life, attempt to learn skills. We of course make mistakes, but if we do not do as well as we would like in one life, we have another chance to do better in another life. If we have hurt somebody, then we realise in the Spiritual World that we love that other soul, whatever we did to them in that life. Our Earth incarnations are about learning to love. So, when we go into a past life that has been unpleasant, there may well be some aspects about it prompting us about how we could learn to love more fully in our present life. The past life is there to help us so that we can live our present life with more love. We can welcome it, rather than be anxious. One of our tasks as a human being is to breathe through fears, and to let them go.

All of us need to manage our own emotions. There will be aspects of us eager to find out about our past lives while other parts of us pull back from them. We need to listen to those different aspects of our self and be with what we are feeling. It could be that we feel warm and open in our hearts, but we could feel a knot of fear in our stomach. Generally, if we feel fear like that, it is actually an indication that we need to go ahead with the experience, that we will learn a lot by going into that past life. We just need to be brave enough.

The experience of going into a past lifetime which is unpleasant can be unsettling. The person you were then can exhibit behaviour and attitudes that are different to who you are now. There are reasons that you behaved the way you did in that life: you could have been beaten, abused or neglected as a child and this may have been too much for you; you could have learnt to behave that way by modelling those around you as a child and repeating their poor behaviours when you were older; you may not have had access to the inner resources to do anything any differently.

Reliving a past life experience where you hurt somebody or even killed them can feel horrible. Whether you have been a victim or perpetrator, this can also lead to a great outpouring of emotion. As you experience those memories, your energy system releases the emotions and drama that are involved. It may not all be pleasant, but it will pass. It is safe for you to experience these traumas because you are channelling an experience from the past. You are not experiencing what is happening today. This will be clear to you.

In this past life, you feel an intimate connection with the person that you were, even if you don't like what they have done, and even though you may have grown a lot since. The connection is still there, and it feels like the connection with your childhood memories as an adult. You could feel confronted if you realise that in some ways you are continuing to repeat some of the patterns of the past life today, but that insight will help you to understand how you need to direct your life now.

If during regression you experience troubling feelings from the past life memories, you must let those feelings out and expunge them from your system. Doing this enables you to feel lighter and freer. As humans, we are basically beings of love and for you to have hurt another human being in a past life or to have been hurt by them feels wrong, and you will want to do something to put things right. Fortunately, within the structure of the past life regression process, there are ways how you can do that.

After you leave the physical body at the end of your past life and ascend to the Light, it is immensely healing to feel your heart open fully. In the Spiritual World, it is possible to meet those souls who hurt you and the ones you hurt. They will not be violent anymore and be much more at peace. But it will be necessary to experience the relationship truthfully and to own the dynamics of what had happened in the past life. This may not be easy at first, because facing difficult situations needs courage. However, you are now meeting that other soul with your heart open, and they will have their heart much more open too. This is a space where healing can occur.

You need to express your truth to this other soul, and in return to listen to them. If they have hurt you, tell them and assert that they had no right to do that. On the other hand, if it was you who did the hurting, you need to ask for forgiveness. This is exceedingly humbling. Within this atmosphere of love, it is likely you are forgiven, then the blockage in your heart relating to that past life can be cleared. A tremendous outpouring of fear and other stuck energy can occur, and you will feel much better, and the love from your heart will be able to flow much easier.

Once the repressed feelings come out into the open, it is clear that these are feelings you have been carrying in the present life too. Therefore, by healing the past life you also heal the present. It all comes together so that you can experience a lot of peace.

It may have taken some bravery for you to take that leap of faith to allow yourself to go into this not-so-nice past life. But once it has been done, the results can be tremendous. You learn a lot about yourself. One thing you could do to help rebalance is to pick up a cushion and put the energy of your past life self into it. Imagine love passing through your hands to your past life self. As our past life self is taking in that love, we are giving that love to ourselves. We feel peace.

Why do people often claim past lives as notable people, but not chamber maids or street sweepers?

It is often suggested that when people talk about their past lives, they have said they were someone famous. If that is the case, doing so would inflate the ego of the person concerned – but how true would it be? Such experiences can be easily ridiculed by others and can give a false impression of regression. In my experience, this is rarely the case. In all the thousands of people whom I have regressed, it has been rare for me to find anyone experiencing the lifetime of some historically significant person. More likely, people experience themselves being someone quite ordinary such as a peasant in the village, a soldier, or a beggar on the street. This is much more realistic.

Often so-called ordinary lives can have a lot of challenges and inner dilemmas for the soul. They may not be as glamor-ous as a life in royalty, but they can be greatly meaningful. Even in the rare instances where someone does access a lifetime, say, of being a figure of royalty or someone else who is gaining a lot of public attention, these lives are not necessarily easy ones. They are certainly not as attractive as we might imagine from being an outsider to such an experience. People who live incarnations of royalty may feel very isolated and trapped by the duties they must fulfil. As children, they would be unlikely to have other children with whom they could play. For most of the time, they would have to be dressed up and look the part for others. Their lives are likely to be unhappy and unfulfilled.

Our souls are not searching for fame or glory. Our souls want to learn humble lessons of life. The lives that we choose reflect that deeper quest for inner growth. In one life, if we experience an incarnation where we are rich and have some fame, then in the next lifetime we could be poor and with few possessions. As souls, we mature by embracing all aspects of human experience. We could choose a life where we live through to old age and another where we die young. In terms of personality, we could choose one life where we have very assertive traits, an ability to strive for what we want, whereas in another life our tendencies may be to be passive and yielding to what others want from us. In all these lives there are learning opportunities and chances for us to grow as souls through our willingness to embrace fully the type of life that is presented to us.

When we go into regression, our ego has no control over what experience will come to us. Our soul presents experiences that offer inner learning and growth; our ego tends to be concerned with self-glorification and keeping things within the boundaries of what we know. Past life regression is a spiritual experience for us to become acquainted with our soul. Our ego is best staying out of the way and being a non-interfering witness and learning from our soul through cooperation.

What sort of past lives can we have, and where do they take place?

There are many types of lives that can emerge from within our consciousness. One of the first things we notice as we enter regression is that we can be male or female. This just needs to be accepted. The soul learns different lessons from one sex to the other. Being male, we are likely to express qualities, capabilities and dispositions that contrast with lives where we are female. Women can bear children. Men tend to be bigger and physically stronger. Both sexes have their worth, and as souls we need to learn to appreciate that and find balance in our attitude towards lives of each sex.

Every type of situation in which we could be born has its potential learning for us. Our past lives could extend over a whole range of possibilities: we can have been rich or poor, a sensitive Native American or healer, an arrogant businessman or a slave being tortured. Our past life could be as a beggar in the street, a soldier or a simple woman doing domestic duties in a house. In an inspiring life we could have been a compassionate leader, or someone who is very loving and helpful to others. We could go from a regression from thousands of years ago to one from comparatively recent times. There are of course, lots of other possibilities as well.

Some of us have ideas about how many lifetimes we have lived, or that we like to think we are old souls having lived many times in all sorts of places. We could also imagine that we have just had a few past lives. The imagination of our normal consciousness does not have an accurate idea about this. It is only as we open our consciousness to our soul, that we begin to unfold a more truthful assessment of who we are and where we have come from. Generally, this is only revealed to us gradually. Often, people greatly underestimate the number of past lives that they have had.

There are lots of possibilities for where your past lives can come from. One lifetime can follow another within months or just a few years. But some souls can also choose to have long periods in the Spiritual World or elsewhere before they incarnate on Earth.

Sometimes, people access lifetimes from cultures that our historians know little about. These types of lifetimes can shed interesting speculations about the history of the Earth. We do not have to have had just human lives on Earth.

I have come across people who have accessed lives as nature spirits, fairies, and other forms of mythical beings. Lives of this type can be very meaningful for those accessing them. Usually, such beings have a great love for the Earth and nature. People feel this love very intensely when they channel these experiences.

I have also come across people who have accessed past lives as animals. It seems that sometimes souls choose to live as an animal in order to experience the consciousness and instinctive drives that particular animal can express. Also, a soul can choose to be in animal form to associate with a human soul whom they love. It could be that a person has lived a past life where they were separated from other people, and they could only have an animal as company. This animal could give love and comfort to that person that could enrich their life. For a human soul to take an animal form in such a life may be a great act of service.

Other people feel that they do not belong on Earth and find that they have lived past lives elsewhere. The consciousness on those other worlds can be vastly different from here on

Earth. They could exist as part of a collective, or in a lifetime with a technological focus where there is little feeling. Maybe they access a life where there is a great deal of spiritual awareness, or one with they are simple organisms living a limited existence. There are so many possibilities.

There are also lifetimes that souls can go through that are not based upon physical worlds at all. These experiences may be mental worlds or energy worlds, where there are contrasting energies providing a focus for learning and activity. However, these experiences can be quite different from what we are used to on Earth. We may go onto such worlds to develop skills or to meet and work with other souls whom we know. Sometimes our experiences on such worlds give us inclinations and capabilities that we can apply in our lives when we are on Earth. For instance, we may learn on a mental world how to focus our thoughts to manifest other energies through our intentions and the power of our minds. This could then be a skill that we can use later in a life on Earth.

How do past lives affect us today?

There are many ways how the past life experiences can impinge upon our life today. In a class I facilitated many years ago, I worked with a woman whose father was an alcoholic. She had an exceedingly difficult relationship with her father due to this condition. It was her dear wish to find peace with him so that she would not carry resentment and hatred around his influence upon her. She carried the same genes as her father, and she had fought with herself during her life so that she would not become an alcoholic like he had been. She felt moved to try regression to explore if she could find relief and understanding.

As she entered her past life, she found that she was a man, and it soon became clear this man was also an alcoholic. To her horror, she realised that he had a son who was very affected by his alcoholism. He was in a large room when noticed his son quivering with fear at the other end of the room while he was exceedingly drunk and angry. The polarity of how the past life mirrored her present life offered this woman a tremendous healing insight. In her present life, roles had reversed. In the past life, her present-life father had been her son. Suddenly, my class participant felt a great rush of compassion for her father's soul. She knew then how all this had come to be.

The way past life problems can work their way out in the present life is usually called karma. Before we are born, we may plan out on a spiritual level how disturbances we have had in the past can be balanced during the lifetime to come. There are many ways karma can express itself, and some of these ways can be quite subtle. It does not necessarily need to be an eye for an eye or anything quite so direct, but distortions have to be worked out. For instance, if in one life a soul kills another soul, in another incarnation it may be arranged for this soul to dedicate himself to helping the other soul, so this soul can find life and purpose. The act of finding value in this other soul's life may go a long way towards balancing the past situation where he killed the other soul. In this situation, compassion balances the cruelty and lack of care that existed earlier.

Karma does not imply that because you are having a challenging life now that you must have been a bad person in a past life. It could be that you have taken on a difficult life to give you the best chance of learning some tough soul lessons so you can grow. There can be many deeper reasons for what we experience, and it is not always obvious what those reasons are.

Sometimes, residues from past lives can exist as fears in our system that need to be faced so that they can be overcome. For instance, someone may experience fear and panic about going into water, and they avoid water, so they do not feel discomforted. Perhaps the fear and panic are because of that soul having drowned in a past life. It can be very therapeutic then for that person to undergo a regression where they can access the drowning, to let the emotion of it go. As, that soul leaves the body, they are putting that trauma behind them. They feel peace as they ascend to the Light. The fear of water, after that, is greatly lessened.

How does our energy body link with regression?

Permeating our physical body is an energy body that connects with the more subtle dimensions of who we are. To illustrate this, if you suffer from an emotional loss, you are likely to feel that as a pain in your heart. It is likely this has little to do with the working of your physical heart and is much more to do with your energy heart, which feels love and loss acutely. The heart energy centre is situated in the middle of your chest, so this is where you feel that pain. We have lots of energy centres that link to areas of our physical body. When we go into an altered state of consciousness to access the memory of a past life, we might not be aware of our physical body. The inner reality that we access connects with our energy body, not the physical one.

The memories of past lives can express themselves powerfully through the mechanism of our energy body. If we have a trauma from a past life, a trauma that was not resolved at the time, then there may be some residues of that affect our energy system today. For instance, a person who was strangled or hung in a past life may feel a tenderness around their neck and feel extremely sensitive about anyone touching or approaching that part of their body. This can occur without there being any direct connection to a known event in their present life.

I used to give presentations about past lives to large groups of people, quite regularly when I lived in Scotland. At the end of one of these, I offered to do a brief demonstration to show how regression worked. There was a woman in the audience, quite eager to come forward as a volunteer. Within moments of guiding her into the experience of regression, she began to clutch at her neck and gave the appearance of gasping for air. She was doing this spontaneously without me having suggested anything to induce it. Her body was writhing, as if in terror and pain. I asked her to tell me what she was recalling. She said she was being strangled.

I was a little embarrassed that this should happen in front of all these people, but I had to go through it with her, had to guide her through to her death where her consciousness left her body. Once the trauma was over, she could feel safe. She felt sad for her body, but she was not in it anymore and she was free from that distress. It took her a while for it all to settle. I asked questions to encourage her to explain the setting about the man who had strangled her. This felt necessary for the grounding of the experience. It was not quite the type of regression experience that I had expected to share with this audience, however I had a responsibility to ensure that this woman was feeling OK before she left me.

A couple of years later, I had a stall for my work at that same venue. At some point in that day, a woman approached me.

She told me that she was the one who had been a subject for that demonstration. I had not remembered her. Then she thanked me. All her life, she had worn scarves and had not been able to let anyone touch or get anywhere near to her neck. After the brief regression, all that tenderness had completely disappeared. Now she felt quite at ease around her neck and the discomfort had gone.

How many past lives can we have?

When I guide people into a regression session, I generally work with the person's memory of one lifetime at a time. Unless it is a short, uneventful life, there is usually much to be explored, experienced, and understood from the regression to one lifetime without overlapping into others. I prefer my clients to experience one lifetime thoroughly and integrate the learning from that before going onto another one. This approach to past life therapy does not lend itself so easily to discovering how many lifetimes people have in their memory.

There are approaches I can use though when I have clients who are interested in discovering answers to these types of questions. I can ask the inner consciousness of my client to go to the first human lifetime that they have had on Earth. Some people have had their first incarnation in Palaeolithic times, in a hunter and gatherer setting or with some ancient civilisation that is unknown by historians. Others find themselves in a tribal society, or in more known historical situations such as ancient Egypt, China, or India. There are also those whose first lifetimes as humans on Earth places them somewhere from comparatively recent times, say, in the last few hundred years. Some even discover that their first human life on Earth is the one that they are living now.

For me to ask: 'What is your first human life on Earth?' is not necessarily the end of the story. If I ask the inner consciousness of my client to go to the first lifetime that they have had on Earth, they might find that they have lived a non-human lifetime that predates their first human incarnation "on Earth. Then, if I ask their consciousness to experience their first physical incarnation, they may find themselves living as another sort of being on another world than Earth. To go even further, if I ask their inner consciousness to go to their first experience as a soul, this can give some beautiful rudimentary experiences of love and Light from within the Spiritual World.

The evolution that we each take as souls can have so many different pathways. For souls who are quite young, the kind of lifetimes they experience tend to consist of those with simple themes and perhaps one main soul lesson to be learnt. Very often, souls having their first lives on Earth choose lives where they need to focus upon survival and use their strength to achieve that. Having a life with a survival theme give that soul grounding and the strength to use their will in subsequent lives. For souls who are very developed, the type of lifetimes they have can be immensely complex and multidimensional, with many layers and needs calling to be fulfilled. It is also possible with mature, developed souls, that they have more than one life concurrently. There is quite a mix of souls on Earth. Souls are attracted to the diversity of opportunities on our world.

It is almost impossible to gain a definitive answer about how many lifetimes have been lived. Certainly, if a soul is having their first incarnation, this is clear. Also, if a soul is finding their way with the early stages of their evolution, it may be possible to count the number of incarnations that have been lived. But beyond that, it can become less certain and more conjecture. Most people tend to underestimate the numbers of lifetimes that they have lived. They can confine their count to a select number but then an unusual thought or image come into their consciousness, and they become aware of a series of other lives that they had not considered.

Some souls also tend to allow large spaces between the timing of one incarnation after another, while others prefer short intervals from one lifetime to the next. This is an individual process. We all have our own pathways. Hence, there may be some souls who have been around for a long while who have not incarnated very often, while there are other souls crowding in their lives to gain as much Earthly experience as possible.

There are many questions that can't be answered definitively. Is there more than one universe? Does our soul live in a multidimensional reality where many lifetimes and experiences can occur simultaneously? What dimensions exist in the Spiritual World? There is much about our existence as souls that is a great mystery.

Why do some people access past lives and others don't?

The way consciousness is structured varies from one person to another; there are genetic variations. For example, in a family some family members could inherit a psychic gift, an openness to experience the Spiritual Worlds, and this trait is passed down through the generations. They are able to easily recall their past lives, often without having any formal regression sessions. On the other hand, there are other people whose rational critical mind dominates their consciousness. For such people, to access their past lives may be quite a challenging task, even with a skilled regression therapist. Their minds are more directive rather than being receptive.

From a spiritual perspective, the soul chooses the type of family into which it is born. A soul may decide to be in a family with a psychic disposition so that we can develop spiritual connection, and to serve people with this gift. However, if there are people around us in our family or group who are critical, we may suppress our spiritual gifts because of fear of ridicule or rejection. There could be some member of our family who has had a difficult experience due to the expression of their spiritual nature. They then could decide that it is safer for themselves and other members of their family if this capacity is denied. In these circumstances, we need to be brave to assert the true qualities that comprise who we are, rather than living an inauthentic life. It may be part of our spiritual path learn how we can release fears within us that prevent us from expressing our truth.

Another path we could choose would be to be in a family where the members of that family have little inclination towards opening their spiritual faculties. This predisposition could stem from the family genetic make-up. However, the psychology and belief structures of various individuals within the family could be also opposed towards any kind of spiritual openness. The soul may have a path where their purpose is to open to their spiritual faculty. However, in such a family, it is hugely difficult to do so. It is necessary for that soul to rise out of the pressures of conforming to that family's patterns of existence, and to find their own independent path. This takes a great deal of strength and courage. The soul needs to work through layers of their personality to find their own connection to Spirit. Perhaps there is a catalyst like a personal tragedy that drives the person towards a transformation where they can listen directly to their soul rather than their personality. If they can succeed with this soul challenge, they may not only liberate themselves, but also other members of their family.

A person may have spiritual gifts in their life today. However, this does not imply that they are a more spiritually developed soul than one who displays less in the way of spiritual gifts. Some highly developed souls choose quite simple and humble souls. They may be hardly noticed. Whatever are our gifts, our responsibility is to do the best that we can with those gifts. It is not for us to judge others. We need to be true to our own path. We cannot know all that there is to know about all souls.

What benefits are there in remembering our past lives?

There is some innate force in us that propels us to learn who we are, and to know about what our essence is. The impulse that inspires us to discover who we are from within is that same force that drives scientists, explorers, philosophers, mystics, and innovators. The Greeks wrote at the Temple of Delphi that the aim of human existence was to 'know thyself'.

What we experience through our external senses of the world around us is only one aspect of our existence. Our inner awareness also matters. To discover what is within us gives meaning and adds an inner context to our lives.

A lot of the feelings and thoughts of our lives comes from belief systems we have acquired from earlier in our lives. We can behave in certain ways without understanding why we do so. Much of our consciousness is hidden in deep layers of our awareness. To learn about these layers can give us more control over our responses and reactions. For instance, as a child someone may have shouted and make us feel frightened. We may want to curl into a ball and shut out the world. It may seem too much for us, so that we bury all the feelings deep inside, and not want to feel it anymore. But then, when we are older, someone else may shout at us and the memory of when we were little might take over and we may want to curl into a little ball and hide away just like we did as a child. Our adult self may want to stand up and be assertive towards the person shouting at us, but the feelings of our child self is persuasive. If we can be brave enough to go within ourselves to that childhood memory, we can allow those frightening feelings to be cleansed from our system. We can give love to our child self, and then those early memories no longer affect us. That is what can happen with a childhood memory, but there are layers of our inner consciousness that go beyond our present lifetime. When we go to deeper layers of our consciousness and memories that extend also into our past lives, we learn about the history of our soul and begin to free ourselves from traumatic residues and limiting beliefs that we do not need anymore.

For us to learn about our inner self is as much a valid activity as singing, dancing, walking, painting, or any activity that we would regard as being natural and intrinsic to who we are and what we do as human beings. It is an activity of self-exploration that is a great resource that we can tap into. We are still discovering the potentials of what we can discover by engaging in meditation and inner work.

Through religious dogma, people have been dissuaded from learning about their inner self. Many religions have developed intolerance to belief systems that differ in any way from how they interpret sacred scriptures. Groups engaging in any forms of spiritual practice that venture outside what religions regard as acceptable have been called heretics. Many have suffered because of this. Through the ages, people have developed fear about what is deep inside each of us, and it's a fear of the unknown. These fears have been largely baseless and have kept us from undertaking inner exploration where we could discover precious and wonderful aspects about who we are.

To gain the benefits of past life regression, we need to meet these fears with courage. There are some people for whom doing past life regression does not feel right. However, if your intuition suggests it, then there could be some great and healing experiences awaiting you. These could assist you to find purpose and meaning in your life, in addition to spiritual fulfilment.

By going into the Spiritual World during a regression session, we also have the opportunity to use our intuition in ways that we do not have with our normal consciousness in our everyday life. We sense the inner freedom we have in the Spiritual World. Our intuition is a faculty for us to know what is true and right for us to do. By experiencing our soul exercising this skill in the Spiritual World, it helps to open our capacity for expressing intuition with our everyday life on Earth too.

What is the history of Past Life Regression?

In the known civilisations of many of the Eastern religions, the concept of reincarnation is central to their beliefs. There are sources indicating this going back many thousands of years. The ancient Hindu texts of the Upanishad formed a basis for Buddhist and Hindu thought, and very clearly included teachings about reincarnation.

Although there are no written records to confirm this, it is conceivable that some Indigenous tribes were open to belief in reincarnation. Their knowledge was passed down orally and the shaman of the tribe attained many varieties of spiritual experience. In the Western spiritual traditions, Ancient Greek and Egyptian mystery schools appear to show practices supporting the theory of reincarnation existed within the priesthood and temple culture. Even in Christianity, there are scholars who postulate that there are allusions to reincarnation, such as when John the Baptist is purported to be a reincarnation of Elijah.

Some have suggested that Bible texts may have been tampered with in the Council of Nicaea held in 325AD. This was the first ecumenical council of the Christian church, presided over by Emperor Constantine I. Therefore, there are suspicions about how authentic the original scriptures remained after these meetings. Sadly, there were numerous deliberately lit fires in ancient libraries that destroyed huge amounts of written records of ancient philosophy, history, and information about religious movements from early times. Many priceless treasures of our early ancestors and how they viewed our human existence have been lost. It means that accurate knowledge about early belief in reincarnation in European countries is largely speculative, as are the practices people may have engaged in to encourage past life recall.

In more recent times, since the late 1880s, there has been a resurgence of interest in reincarnation. This coincides with the rapid increase in trade and cultural exchanges that was occurring between the East and West. Interest in the concept of reincarnation spread to the West from the East through organisations like the Theosophical Society. In the early 1900s, Sigmund Freud experimented with regression work with his work on psychoanalysis. He investigated the depths of the human mind, and how hidden neurosis that people carry when brought to conscious awareness, could bring about healing. Carl Jung went further, exploring how the human psyche could have a spiritual dimension that linked us together. He called this the 'collective unconscious'.

Another pioneer was Edgar Cayce. During the 1920s and '30s, Edgar Cayce was able to channel detailed information through his Higher Self to help people with medical problems, and to help develop their awareness of their souls. The information he channelled was recorded. Cayce himself had no conscious memory of what he channelled and was in a state of deep trance. However, in the soul readings, he spoke about people's past lives and did this in a way to offer people psychological help as well as knowledge of their essential being.

Interest in the workings of the mind grew during the early twentieth century and many approaches to psychotherapy developed. Linked with this, there was also an interest in hypnotism. In 1956, there was a famous book published called *In Search of Bridey Murphy* by Morey Bernstein. In this book, Bernstein, who was an established hypnotherapist, wrote about how he hypnotised Ruth Simmons. Bernstein gained detailed information from Ruth while she was in trance, about the lifetime of Bridey Murphy, who purportedly lived in the 1800s. The book was a sensation, and later was made into a film. From this time onwards, past life regression became a field of endeavour on its own. Therapists began to work with Age Regression – a technique to bring forth memories not only from early childhood but also past lives. Two pioneers in this field were Denys Kelsey and Joan Grant, and their work was important. They reported that people were able to remember the time of their conception and concluded that we all have the capability to function and record events even in the absence of a physical body. The notion that we had the capacity to do this was a turning point in past life therapy.

After this, many eminent past life therapy specialists appeared, and during the 1970s and '80s, there were numerous innovative books produced. Ian Stevenson pioneered the research related to spontaneous recall of past lives, particularly in children. Other authors included Helen Wambach, Edith Fiore, Morris Netherton, Thorwald Dethelfsen, Chet Snow and many others. My own teacher, Dr Roger Woolger, wrote his own seminal work, *Other Lives, Other Selves* in 1988.

In recent times, mention needs to be made of the immense contribution made by Dr Brian Weiss. His book *Many Lives, Many Masters* has become a modern-day classic and is the most widely read book about past life regression Therapy. He teaches and runs courses around the world. Dr Michael Newton is another outstanding pioneer. Dr Newton developed techniques for people to access memory of being and awareness about the development of the soul in the Spiritual Worlds. His brilliant books include *Journeys of Souls* and *Destiny of Souls*. As I have mentioned earlier, I have been privileged to have trained with his institute, The Newton Institute, and to become a qualified practitioner of his method.

PAST LIFE THEMES

THEMES AND SETTINGS

The past lives that people access can present in a myriad of guises and historical periods. The past life setting is like clothing for the memory of the experience. We may be in a battle, living a simple life on a farm, in some noble court or as a homeless person on the street – and these are just a few of the possibilities. For the person regressing, the setting is of great interest and of central importance, but for the soul, the outer appearances matters much less. What is more crucial for the soul is how a person deals with challenges and dilemmas in that lifetime. The setting of the lifetime gives grounding to lessons in the current lifetime.

Even though we are all on individual paths, there are some basic human lessons that we all have to encounter at some point on our soul journeys. How and when we attempt these lessons is different for each soul. For some of us, getting through these fundamental lessons may be easy, while other souls may struggle with them. Some of these lessons may need many lives to go through all the intricacies and to test our capability sufficiently because the soul wants to know that we have the strength and awareness to manage all aspects of a particular lesson. Progressing spiritually gives the soul joy. If we do not complete the learning of a particular soul lesson in one lifetime, then we incarnate again later with a similar purpose. We keep trying until we master the lesson.

Some universal soul themes appear in people's regressions quite frequently. With each of these themes there are tasks and challenges that the soul needs to meet with integrity. As we gain understanding about the kinds of conditions we can face as humans on Earth, then this helps us develop a sense of responsibility for the life we live.

SURVIVAL

Often when people do regression for the first time, they access a lifetime where the issue of survival is of great importance. Having to apply energy to survive helps us to acquire inner strength so we can cope on our own. This is often played out in the relationships we choose in life.

There are people we love and who love us. We can easily get into patterns of depending on our loved ones, feeling that we can only manage when we have those souls with us. However, as well as learning to love we also need to express our individuality. A stage in our development is when we learn to stand on our own feet and to shine our own Light. There is a yearning in us to feel that uniqueness and to express who we are to the full, and if we are consistently bound up too much with others this may hold us back. Hence, there is probably one lifetime or more where we choose circumstances to be largely living on our own. This could be in a scenario where we become separated from others. Without other people around us, we face the prospect of loneliness and face inner questions about how much we want to live. Our soul wants us to succeed, however our emotions, thoughts and desires may feel the urge to give up. If the conditions are challenging, then we need to work hard psychologically and apply our will to survive. With no human support, we may need to open to nature and feelings of inner connection that we can sense with other lifeforms around us. This simple incarnation could be a lifetime where find peace through simple rhythms and being in our own company. If we struggle to cope being so much on our own, this could be an experience where we falter. If we falter, then we may feel disappointed when the lifetime is over. There will be opportunities for us to attempt the lesson again in another time.

In a survival lifetime we may get used to being on our own. When our body dies and we rise to the Spiritual World, it may take a while for us to open our consciousness to other souls again. But when we adjust and open our hearts there might be a large gathering of souls in the Spiritual World to meet us with their love. We welcome the feeling of being loved after such a life on our own.

Such lives are good foundations for our soul to grow and progress. Souls do not always choose lives where they are on their own for their growth. There are those who willingly retreat into lives on their own because they want to escape from other people. Sometimes when souls have been hurt by others, they might decide that it is easier for them to stay away from people than to face the possibility of enduring pain again. Those souls may be running away from life and hiding from the world and seeking safety and security by being on their own. This may be not such a beneficial choice. We do not grow through repeating a similar experience of isolation. Doing this can entrench this pattern and make it harder for us to open our hearts to others. This does not help us at all.

While we are on Earth, most of our soul lessons are centred around our relationships with other humans.

PERSECUTION AND INJUSTICE

Another theme is persecution and injustice. You may visit a lifetime where you were a healer or humanitarian engaged in helping people to improve their lives. You may have even been a leader offering spiritual teaching. When you lived a such a life of service and compassion this would have brought about wonderful feelings of joy and fulfilment. But you could not control how others would react to you. Others may not like what you do and the attention you receive and feel jealousy or envy. There could even be religious intolerance in the society around you. Others may feel bewildered by the Light you emit and feel threatened by it. Even though your actions are good they may not be appreciated by others. This could lead to situations where you are hurt or persecuted. On a soul level, this would be a test for you and them. You may have been subjected to torture, abuse and a painful death, situations that were particularly challenging to withstand, and you may have been in a position where there was little you could do about the suffering you experience.

Perhaps you were accused of being a witch. In that life, you may have been a simple herbalist wanting to help people. But you may have been burned at the stake or drowned. There are other expressions of persecution that can be just as violent.

These can be emotional experiences for people doing regression to go through. You may need to cleanse yourself of the massive fear associated with these memories. There can be lots of tears and energetic sensations. In such cases, you need to be channels to allow yourself to release the emotion and painful thoughts that come forth, without resistance. When these residues are fully liberated, you will feel much lighter. As a therapist, I always need a good box of tissues ready for these types of lives.

At the end of a persecution life, leaving the body is a tremendous relief. Going to the Spiritual World is enormously welcomed. Often, there are Spirit Beings offering healing that is needed for the soul to help recover from the trauma. In the Spiritual World there may be an occasion to meet with other souls who were involved in the persecution. Honest communication is needed so both sides can reach understanding.

In this present life a person may have wanted to do healing or help others, like they did before, but they are afraid of the exposure and how others would react, due to past lifetimes of persecution. The fear would repulse them from going into a situation where something similar could happen again. By accessing these lives, it can alleviate these problems.

In terms of soul lessons, going into a lifetime of persecution is a test of commitment and faith. The soul needs to be steadfast in their beliefs and feel the worthiness of what they are doing. Facing persecution can result in reactions of feeling disillusioned, bitter, and angry and sometimes vengeful. Souls need to be strong to hold their line amid the challenges presented by persecution.

Sometimes a soul goes into a lifetime of persecution because of karma stemming from some previous lifetime where they have been intolerant or tortured others. This life is then about bringing a balance to feel what it is like to be a victim, and to learn about the futility of bringing suffering to others. If a soul reacts to persecution with anger and thoughts of vengefulness and this becomes entrenched, then these responses can generate a cycle of lives as victim followed by perpetrator. This cycle only ends by the soul releasing that hate and anger and finding acceptance.

Some souls are willing to engage in the hard work of healing others, whatever the cost, because they feel that this is what they need to do. They may do this life after life, acting from a place of inner devotion and unconditional love. In this there are some rewards. It is always gratifying to return to the Spiritual World after a life like this, and to meet with other souls who have received healing and help. The person in this life is incredibly grateful, and the healing soul receives a lot of love for all the good that they have done.

SACRIFICE

The sacrifice theme is similar to the persecution theme but with some subtle differences. Whereas persecution lives are ones where the soul strengthens their faith and commitment, sacrifice lives are about learning self-love.

In ancient societies human sacrifice was quite common. These rituals were performed to please the Gods in a plea that there could be better harvests. On occasions, the sacrifice could be performed for darker reasons and members of the community would drink the blood of the victim to gain power. Sometimes the victim would be made to feel that they have a special place in the society before then having their life taken from them. Sacrifice would be a horrific way to die. If the ritual of sacrifice was extended the soul would likely be lifted out of the body before it went too far.

People usually access sacrifice lives when they are continuing the pattern of sacrificing themselves in their life today. They could be allowing others to dictate how they should live their lives – at a cost to their own happiness. They are likely to be quite passive, and by not asserting themselves would feel damaged, as if others are treating them as a form of sacrifice. They may believe that their only sense of worth will come about through giving up their lives for others. The imprint of these patterns could repeat themselves over many lifetimes until they are understood, and the soul is ready to let them go. By accessing a sacrifice past life, people can come to understand the limiting pattern and then how it connects with their life today. The challenge is then for the person to assert themselves now, rather than continue to be passive.

I have had clients that have been in situations where their health is suffering and they have continually found themselves driven to acts of self-sacrifice, maybe with their family or their work. They have not been able to control this and needed to discover the source of the pattern in their lives.

It could be most helpful for a victim of sacrifice to meet in the Spiritual World with those souls who brought about the sacrifice. Our essence is love, and everyone is deserving of love and respect. Performing rituals of sacrifice is not respectful to the person who is sacrificed. If you have suffered through being the victim of sacrifice in one or more of your past lives, you need to become aware of your true worth, rather than the diminished sense of worth placed on you from the community members doing the sacrificing.

Your soul may come into a life like this as karma and to balance actions where you have been behaving in a cruel manner to others in earlier lives. Alternatively, your soul may simply wish to come into that lifetime as an endeavour to teach other souls through your own example and innocence about compassion. In whatever way you have approached it, your soul wants to do this to learn greater self-love.

Being a victim in a sacrifice life is just one part of the equation. Even more challenging are lifetimes where you may have been the perpetrator of someone else being sacrificed. These are lives where your heart is closed, and you behaved in a way that was extremely cruel to others. To allow yourself to access such a lifetime can demand considerable courage on your part. It will feel extremely unpleasant to experience your heart being closed and perpetuating acts of cruelty to others. As a therapist, when I deal with such lifetimes, it is vital for my client to trace how they came to close their hearts in that lifetime. Through this they gain understanding that enables them to forgive themselves and resolve not to do it again.

We all have shadow sides to our nature. If we suffer from abuse or loss, our reactions can easily be to close our hearts, shut down our emotions and choose not to care about other people. With our hearts closed, we operate using our desires and calculating will. There is no love or compassion to guide us. Our desire is to relate to others in a similar way to how we were treated. When we regress to the situations where we brought about acute suffering to others, it can be painful because our hearts are open, and we intensely feel the pain that others feel. We feel the closed heart that our past life self had as being foreign to us. It is not a state of being that we want.

However, experiencing this can be healing for we release compassion into our system. When channelling our past life self, we realise that what we were doing with these other people was projecting onto them the hurt that had been buried inside us. In such lives, there is not much love, and we feel isolated and lonely. It gives us some momentary comfort to hurt others, but it does not last.

It can be worse than that. We may reach a stage where we gain pleasure through causing pain to others, even killing them. Feeling that sense of power over others might bring about a surge of energy inside us that becomes addictive. Ultimately this is only a poor substitute for the love that we feel is lacking. These are the darkest kinds of lives that we can go through. They are lives where we have sought power over others to satisfy our desires, but in a way that is totally selfish. The fear that others experience gives us an adrenaline rush, and that is what we live for. As time goes on, we are depleted by this and become incredibly alone.

When we end such a life and leave the body, we feel how much our heart was closed. It is a long passage for us to reach the Light. We may not want to reach the Spiritual World for we know what we have done, and some part of us is aware that in the Spiritual World the Light that is there shines truth upon us and there is no escape. It is a trial for us to confront our actions from that life when we reach the Spiritual World. We feel all the suffering and pain that we directed to others, and we have to meet those souls that we hurt. This is one situation where we need to find much courage.

FEARS AND PHOBIAS

When we sense instinctively that we are in danger, our nervous system contracts in fear and go into overdrive. This is the instinctive response of 'flight or fight'. When fear erupts in our system our behaviour can become erratic and we can lose control of what we are doing. Suddenly, we feel desperate for some form of escape. When we feel such fear, it is difficult to manage those feelings, centre ourselves and use our faith and inner strength to find peace. If we can focus on our breathing, we can steady ourselves. Sometimes, though, the fear may feel too much for us.

In extreme situations of trauma our nervous system is not able to cope, and we experience some form of breakdown. This can be damaging on many levels. If the trauma is prolonged, the harm to our energy body is worse. These are situations that we are not able to process at the time, and we are likely to carry the distortions caused by these traumas through to later stages of our life, and even into the next life.

In your psyche today, you may be carrying fears and phobias that are rooted in past lives. Another one of the themes you may need to address is how you confront those fears. You may need to cleanse yourself of disturbances in your energy system.

For instance, if you have a fear about going into water, you may try to convince yourself that there is no reason to be afraid. You might try to tell yourself that being in water is a beautiful refreshing experience. You may try to use your will to overcome your fear. You also could attempt to ignore the fear. All of this is likely to be of no avail, if the root of the problem goes deeper within you than you can reach. Instinctively you may know that your fears go beyond anything that you have experienced in your present lifetime. You will either seek answers or hide from it.

With being afraid of water, you may have had an experience in your childhood where you fell into a swimming pool before you could swim, or where you were dumped by a wave and rolled around in the surf. These experiences could have caused an extreme reaction and fear. But you might sense that there is more to it. The fear might not match exactly what you experienced as a child. For instance, your fear might be more focused upon being in open water, whereas your childhood experience was in a swimming pool. But the fear is likely to grow and spread anyway. You may not want to go near any kind of water, and even the thought of it may prompt your body to start to perspire and your stomach tighten.

Your inner thoughts may tell you that you must get away from the water, that it is a risk to you. The closer you get to the water, the worse your fear reactions become. Your nervous system will insist that you find safety.

When I work with people experiencing these types of problems, I assure them that whatever happened is in the past and it is not able to hurt them now. I reinforce suggestions that they can safely allow the experience to channel through them. Then I encourage my client to breathe into the part of their body where they feel the fear most strongly.

When they do, they may find that there are memories of a past life that are coming into their awareness. Suddenly they may sense something, like being in cold water. There may be waves crashing around them. Perhaps they have been pushed off a ship, and they are stranded in the middle of the ocean and are fearful and distressed that they are going to die.

Or, a wave might push them underwater, and they struggle to try to get to the surface, and then after a while they cannot try anymore. They may have drowned and leave their body. When the person accesses an experience like this, they feel the panic and the struggling for breath, the terror, but also the peace when they leave the body. They realise that it was not the end. When they go through this two or three times, they feel acceptance and this begins to work through the person's system.

In a past life regression, a story like this comes out with lots of emotion and body reaction. This is a release and letting go of that trauma. It cleanses you and enables you to feel much lighter. The outcome is that you feel liberated and free from that past. This can be an important step in modifying how you approach water. However, it is possible that there could be more layers to the problem that still need attention.

In terms of the past life, there may be elements such as the relationship with the people who pushed you off the ship that need to be resolved. The anger towards those people also needs to be expressed in some way, inwardly, so that it is not held inside anymore. There might be other lives in which you have drowned through slightly different traumas. Some of those lives may need to be visited also until you feel that you can genuinely relax in water and know all those fears are behind you. Your nervous system needs time to adjust so water is considered safe, and it will take a little time to consolidate before your inner beliefs are convinced that you can survive and enjoy being in water. Then you can foresee a future where you can be in water with ease.

There are numerous fears and phobias that exist. Not all of them are from past lives. Some originate from our present life from traumas we have been through. We could even pick up a fear and phobia that has been imprinted inside us from someone else. Perhaps one of our parents has projected their fears onto us, and we have thought that they are our fears. We are sensitive beings, and we are susceptible to all kinds of influences.

Another example. A client and her husband were booked on a flight to go on holiday. They had been anticipating the pleasure of this holiday for a long time. When I listened to my client, her voice was wavering on the phone. She wanted so much to go on this holiday, but she was terrified of the flight.

As my client lay down for her session, her body was shaking slightly, and she was obviously nervous, even though we had done other sessions together before. I asked her to recall a recent time when she had felt fear of going on this holiday. She was able to connect with that, and then tell me where she felt the feelings in her body. Her stomach was knotted with fear. As she breathed into it almost immediately, she experienced herself in a plane. She was a male pilot of a fighter plane in World War II and the plane had been hit. My client was totally immersed in the persona of the fighter pilot. The plane was on fire, and he was desperately trying to bring the plane under control but couldn't and the plane was going down. My client was shouting out and her body was shaking and moving around chaotically.

The pilot was going to die. My client's body was contorted with fear and there was perspiration dripping from her. The plane crashed and he died. He was no longer in his body. It felt slightly better, but she was still shaking from the trauma. As my client connected to her present-life body, she was able to comprehend that her soul had survived that ordeal and that this experience was in the past. It was all over.

Once she had acknowledged what had happened, I guided her back into the trance to go through the fighter pilot's death again. I asked her consciousness to enable her to experience the pilot's death more deeply, and with more detail. She did that, and her body reacted again, but not quite as much as the first time. I guided her to go through that past life death five times. Each time, it got easier for her. With the final recall, she could cope with it quite peacefully and experience herself after the death, ascending to the Light and feeling in her heart the love of many Spirit Beings there to meet her soul. The residues of that trauma had now been dispelled from her system and she felt relaxed and relieved.

The session did not take long, but it had been extremely intense. My client left my consulting room feeling happy and confident. It was some weeks before I heard from her. The next time we spoke, she had returned from her holiday. She and her husband had enjoyed it very much. Her flight had proceeded without incident, and she had felt relaxed throughout.

PAST LIFE POLARITIES

One of the essential soul tasks that we must go through during our evolution is to deal with polarities. By doing this, we develop perspective. If we resist the opportunities of learning through one type of experience, then we may choose a lifetime where we experience the opposite to help open our awareness. As an example, we may go through an incarnation where we have been rich and able to enjoy every material luxury that we could wish for. Perhaps we became lazy in that life, thinking that we are entitled to have those riches. Or, we may have had a rather shallow existence where we were vain and occupied only upon our material wellbeing, with no thought or concern for others. We have probably learnt little through this type of existence. A possible next step for us might be to go into a lifetime where we are poor and perhaps living on the streets; a lifetime where we had to struggle for our existence. We could have accepted these poor conditions and done our best with what we had. There may have been moments of love in this experience, interchanges that gave us simple feelings of happiness. This may have helped us to be able to appreciate that it does not matter how much money we have after all, and that it was the love in our heart that mattered. Our soul could have gained a lot through this response to being poor.

But we might also react adversely to our circumstances and resist suffering through poverty and wish for a different existence. With this attitude, our soul does not learn very much. It could be that we became bitter at having to be poor and decided to give up rather than face the trials that were there. Thus, the necessity of needing to confront themes around being rich and poor would continue until we could find peace and understanding.

Another quite challenging polarity concerns the wish for revenge. Here, two souls may have got caught in a violent struggle that has perpetuated itself for many lives, over several centuries. One of the two souls could have started the cycle through being very hurtful and cruel to the other.

The second soul may have felt so upset and angry about being treated like this that they then vowed revenge so the other one would suffer. If the violence was extreme, then the second soul would likely have felt hatred towards the first and felt with strong venom that they wanted the other soul to suffer in a similar way to how they had suffered.

With that thought, in another lifetime, a scenario may have arisen where the second soul had an opportunity where they could wreak revenge and suffering to the first soul. They could then have been similarly affronted, and then vowed revenge upon the second soul. From this beginning, a cycle of violence can continue repeatedly and the negativity between the two souls continues to build up.

Of course, in the Spiritual World, the two souls would feel love for each other, and they would want desperately to break this cycle so that they could continue to grow and evolve. They would want to be involved with other activities that would help them. This would not be easy. The only way that these souls would be able to break the cycle is for them to continue to be put in situations where they are prompted to initiate violence upon the other until finally one of them grows tired of it. They would have to resist the temptation for revenge, and thus, step out of the pattern. This would be a huge relief for that soul. However, the other one could still feel violent reactions towards anyone who hurts them, but that could be then a pattern that this soul would need to sort out on his own with other souls. The soul with whom he had been perpetuating this pattern would be able to extract himself from this drama to experience other opportunities and move on.

TURN-AROUND LIVES

Before we go into an incarnation, we give ourselves assignments of what we want to learn and how we want to progress as a soul. The tasks we set for ourselves are tests for our character. We plan these tasks for our lifetime on Earth while we are still souls in the Spiritual World. There could be people that come into our lives, situations, or challenges that we need to confront. What we plan in Spirit as a soul is likely to be unknown to us once we are on Earth. We need to tune in deeply to ourselves so that we can identify what we need to do, and to live that truly.

We have the gift of freewill, and we must listen to our heart and intuition to ensure that we carry out the soul plans that are intended for us. With events that take place in our lives which are planned, the test for us is about how we react to those events. If we can act truly then we grow in maturity as a soul. Otherwise, this may be a soul lesson that we need to repeat later.

Another theme is dealing with the pain of loss. It is hard for any of us to cope when a loved one dies or is separated from us indefinitely. Our human self does not want to experience loss; it is utterly disorientating for our security system. However, for our soul, this may well be one of those experiences that we have planned spiritually before we came to Earth as one of our soul lessons.

In a lifetime where we lose a loved one through death or separation, this tests us severely about the meaning and purpose we have in our life. If we loved our partner very dearly, then the shock of the loss affects us tremendously. The loss of our partner at this point may have been what was planned to happen, and our soul challenge is how we react to this death. We may have felt that we wanted to be with our partner all our life or it could have been a dream and what mattered most. We would not want to let go of that dream, or the closeness of our lover.

In a lifetime like this, perhaps we gave up on life and waited to die. From then on, we might have drifted through life never getting close to anyone else. We may have felt that there was too much pain to deal with, and so we decided to bury our emotions and kept them secret. We might even have decided to prematurely end our life by committing suicide so we would not have to live alone.

Alternatively, we might feel angry that our loved one died. It may have felt very unfair that this happened. We could then have closed our heart and gone through life without feeling that we care about anybody or anything. Our blame may have extended to God, and we may have judged that it was all God's fault for allowing this to happen. Therefore, we would react with disbelief and rebellion. Our actions then could become quite destructive, and we might have expressed cruelty to others. We could have been indifferent or dismissive. By the end of our life, when we carry forward this resolve, we would undoubtedly feel isolated and bitter.

Another possibility is that we might have reached out for help, and then gone through a period where we felt tremendously upset and struggled to go on. There may have been spiritual signs of contact from our loved one, but maybe we did not believe that this contact was taking place, whereas if we had then this may have given us hope and helped us. We could have begun to seek answers from Spirit about our partner and have had the wish to gain a deeper sense of spiritual meaning about our existence.

After we grieved and allowed ourselves to receive the love of those around us, we might have felt the need to go on, and to do what we could. We may have sensed that our partner who loved us would have wished us to fulfil ourselves in our life. Therefore, we may then have become open to find happiness with others, even though our partner is no longer there. From this base, we could have eventually found peace. We would still miss our partner, but also feel contentment with what we have done. At the end of that life, we die and meet with the soul of that loved one in Spirit. There is a great feeling of love at reuniting, and we know that love is eternal and that we never lose those whom we sincerely love.

If we had managed to cope and find a viable way forward from this loss, our soul would feel a great sense of accomplishment. This would help us through the loss of our loved one and give us the opportunity to open our heart and love more widely. If the love we felt for our loved one could be redirected and expanded into other forms of expression, then this would help our soul greatly on its path.

On the other hand, if we had given up or closed our hearts, we would likely feel when we entered the Spiritual World, that we had wasted that life. Our test may have been about our need to find inner strength and acceptance because of loss. If we did not find peace from this situation, then as a soul, in the Spiritual World, we feel disappointed. We have missed the opportunity to grow spiritually. Then we would want to go into another life with a similar scenario and try that lesson again. Because we acted in a way that was not conducive to stand on our own feet and to shine our Light after the loss of our partner, we may repeat the same pattern. If we do not learn that lesson the second time, then the feeling of disappointment is be amplified. Then, it may happen again. The pattern of giving up or whatever we have done to avoid dealing with feelings of loss may have become an enduring habit. It may be like a big emotional barrier that feels too difficult for us. Our soul is not satisfied with that. From deep within us, we want to keep repeating lives with that lesson until we sort it out.

Eventually, we hopefully come to a lifetime where, through our soul working extremely hard, we find a way to break the pattern and find a different response to dealing with the situation of loss. There may be the situation again where our loving partner dies. But this time, we may not give up but instead reach out for help, and finally find the means to experience peace, and a future that still has meaning for us. When we reach the Spiritual World after this lifetime, there will be celebrations. At last, we will have learnt this lesson.

This type of life, where after several lifetimes of trying, we overcome a habitual pattern that has been keeping us stuck, is what I would call a turn-around life. We go through many of these types of lives with all sorts of themes. These turn-around lives tend to be the ones where we grow most. We are making a step of growth as a soul that we have not made before. After so much effort, we have finally succeeded with a soul task that has sorely tested us. Such lives are incredibly positive to experience. We will know that our soul has succeeded with an issue that it found exceedingly difficult. This will give us confidence for overcoming challenges that are still outstanding.

SOULMATES AND TWIN FLAMES

Many people feel that there is a special soul who is just for them. If they could find that soul, then in some way, there would be the perfect love. That is the dream. They conceive that this soul would complete them and that by being with that soul, they find union and oneness. Some regard this other soul as a soulmate: a remarkably close soul companion who may have been with you since the beginning of your creation. This soul is the one that you love more deeply and fully than any other soul. A more refined version of this would be to call this soul your twin flame, a soul created from the same essence as you were. At some moment, this essence would have divided somehow to produce your soul and the soul of your twin flame. You feel as though you belong with this other soul, together forever, whatever happens. The two of you sense a feeling of unity only when together. The belief in your twin flame suggests that throughout eternity, whatever you are doing, you are always searching and seeking to be with your twin. You know that when you can be together, only then will you find peace.

People with this belief can become quite obsessed with seeking this special relationship. They might feel as though they know the identity of this soul or are living in hope of finding their other half. Without them, they feel there is something missing inside them. Nothing feels more important than to find resolution around this search for the twin. If you believe that true happiness can only be present when you are with your twin, then this pursuit could easily become the driving force of your existence.

From all my work with thousands of clients, I have come to accept that our spiritual life is a great mystery. So many possibilities and options exist. Love is an energy that has so many dimensions and potentials to it. I feel that twin flames and soulmates do exist. For some people, to seek for a soul love partner can be especially crucial in their life. Love at first sight does happen. It can be a hugely involving and fulfilling experience to meet and be with another soul with whom you feel a deep soul connection. We can learn and gain a lot on our spiritual path through such meetings. When we look into the eyes of such a loved one, the depth of what we perceive can give us a sense of rapture and meaning that we do not feel with others. Our soul companion can be a mirror for us and reflect aspects of our self when we are with them.

There are also some elements of connecting with a close soul companion where we need to be cautious. In our human form, we are largely separated from our Divine consciousness. Because of this, we miss the sense of blissful union that we feel in the Spiritual World. For sensitive souls especially, being on Earth can at times be unbearably lonely. We can seek to recreate this spiritual union somehow.

When sensitive people find another soul whom they know beyond the reaches of this life and into some unfathomable eternity they understand this feeling of knowing them is real. In these instances, if we give our all to this other person and they to us, we may get caught up with this connection. It may become like a protective bubble where we remove ourselves from having a relationship with anyone else, or any other lifeforms around us. We may take refuge in this special relationship so that it becomes isolating. After a while, this is not satisfying. The union that we feel may not be fully what it seems. There could be hidden problems and challenges.

We may have learnt many of the lessons we have needed to go through, whereas our soulmate or twin flame may have not learnt as many lessons – or they may have learnt more. Over time, our interests and potentials may have diverged. When we meet them, even though there is that eternal recognition, it does not mean that we are on a level playing field with them. We might not be so easily able to help our soulmate with their issues, or they with ours. It may mean that in Earthly terms, we are not very compatible. It could mean that we are not able to stay with them, and they need to find some other avenue to learn their lessons.

If we have to part from such a loved soul, we miss them and feel the heartache of their loss terribly. But this may still be necessary, even though we may resist and not want to leave them. This could cause further problems and tangles in our relationship because we may be taking more notice of our desires for them than of our own needs. We need to measure our needs from deep inside our own soul, and not from what we imagine we desire with our soulmate or twin flame.

It could be that with that special soul with whom we are so devoted, that we have been together in many lifetimes, and trust and depend upon each other. However, we may also lean on our soulmate and be dependent upon them which can limit our growth. At some stage in our evolution, we probably need to have some time apart from our loved one just to find our own strength and a sense of who we are as independent beings. We may find it hard, especially when we have been so close to this other soul.

Sometimes with our soulmate or twin flame we can experience jealousy, possessiveness, and power struggles. One of us may have the capacity to be independent more fully than the other. If we experience betrayal by our soulmate or twin flame, we feel this so much more intensely than with anyone else. We may reach a conclusion that we are unable to be without our soul companion. If they have betrayed us, we can feel tremendous hurt and despair. Some souls will rather end their lives than be without their special loved one. This is not such a sensible solution, but for our emotions it could feel like it is the only way possible.

The only way to resolve this dilemma is to broaden our capacity to love. We need to move our attention from our desires to our heart. Then, with our special loved one, we can love them unconditionally and learn to accept them, whatever they do and however they behave. Our faith tells us that we cannot lose them. As souls, we are always connected to them with love, and we will meet them in the Spiritual World. However, there are many other souls for us to love too. spiritual love exists in all life forms, not only this one special soul. If we can allow it, this helps us to build a broader spiritual base to enhance our integrity.

There is one successful pathway for those of us with a twin flame or soulmate. We may, throughout many lifetimes of trials and learning, have grown to support each other with love and acceptance, and become tolerant and open to the needs of others as well. The Light that we share shines more brightly when we are together than when we are on our own. By linking together, we can find ways to be stronger in our love and adherence to Spirit. We may dedicate ourselves to act compassionately and use the tremendous love that exists between us to help others. The combination of our energies has the potential to be a great force for good. The sense of what we achieve together is a love that we can share intensely.

Through love and support towards each other, and with a focus that reaches outwards, we are able grow in our unity and the spiritual work that we do. This brings an ecstatic sense of joy and fulfilment to us.

LIFE REVIEW

We are on a learning path, and that path does not stop when we reach the Spiritual World. It just transcends into less dense layers of vibration. When we are in the Spiritual World, our heart is radiant. Our energy field is acutely sensitive to feelings and thoughts. We are able to remember all the details of the physical lifetime that we lived and go through a process of review. As souls, it is natural that we want to have done well in a lifetime, and that we have been true to our path. If we have strayed from what we intended to do, we may feel quite afraid of facing ourselves. Our Guides and Higher Beings are compassionate and will try to help us. If the lifetime has been much less than we hoped in terms of our accomplishment, no one will be more disappointed in it than us. We will have to come to terms with what we have done or omitted.

When we meet souls that we have hurt in our physical life, we have to acknowledge it with them; they will know. When our heart is open it feels almost unbearable that we could have hurt them. From that place of love in the Spiritual World, all we want to do is be kind and compassionate to all living beings, and we feel our loving connection with all forms of life. This could be a considerable contrast with how we felt while we were still on Earth. We may want to ask those souls for forgiveness, which will be very emotional for us to do. The other souls will perceive our actions for what they were. Unless we choose to turn away, we will recognise what is true. There will be knowledge and awareness in the space between us and the other souls. Mostly, unless there is some attachment or unresolved agenda, the other souls will forgive us, and this will bring a great relief. When people experience one of these processes during regression, there can be lots of tears. But the challenge is not so much to accept others' forgiveness, but for us to be able to forgive our self.

When we are not able to forgive ourselves, then we are inclined to want to punish ourselves in subsequent lives, feeling that this is what we deserve. We may believe that we are not a good person, and then carry those feelings of unworthiness when we go into lives on Earth. This does not help us grow. Eventually, we need to put our mistakes behind us. All souls make mistakes. To be human means we are not perfect in our physical lives. When what we have done is over and in the past, we do not need to hang onto it anymore. Our task is to assimilate it, learn from it and to let it go. Only when we are willing to do that are we able to love ourselves and love others in the fullness that we can.

SOULS WHO COMPLETE THEIR TIME ON EARTH

As souls gain experience on Earth and accomplish their inner goals, they grow in maturity, evolving over many lifetimes. Eventually, they may reach the point where they can complete their human incarnations and no longer need to return. This is a moment of great celebration and freedom for a soul. The Spiritual World is such a multidimensional reality that there are numerous options for what souls choose to do next. Some may want to become Spiritual Guides or Healers, while others teach or study. There are also great possibilities to create or explore. Some souls, even though they do not have to, choose to return for another human incarnation on Earth.

Occasionally, I have met and worked with people who have discovered that they do not need to be on Earth anymore and have chosen to be here rather than remain in the

Spiritual World. They will be on Earth because they choose to be here, because they have volunteered. Typically, in some ways, it has been a surprise for these people to learn of this, although, in another way, they have already known. It is a great moment of spiritual awakening when they become aware of their true, authentic identity, and they can find profound peace. They will have no karmic obligations, no duties or entanglements. Such people will be human, with emotions and thoughts, but deep inside them there will be quietness that nothing on Earth can disturb.

There are many people that have said to me that this will be their last life on Earth. Some of them are probably wanting to escape. Others may feel that they have had enough. But just because people have the thought that they have no more Earth lives to live, does not mean that this will be true. Reaching the attainment where a soul no longer needs to return to Earth is because of a huge amount of spiritual endeavour. We cannot make it happen with our will.

I once had a client who regressed to a past life as a woman in Russia. In this life, her father was abusive and cruel. He drank too much and did not look after himself. This man was hard and not approachable. His behaviour was enough to affect his daughter adversely. When her father was dying, it was a relief for her that he was going. She was at his bedside. However, when he died, she saw the energy of his soul, and it shot upwards with tremendous rapidity. Immediately his soul was gone. She was puzzled. But then, later, when she died and went to the Spiritual World, she could not find the soul of her father. It was later that she realised that this was his last life. He would not need to come to Earth anymore. He had not lived a life that seemed 'good' or spiritual. What he had lived out was experiences that he had to go through to balance the other experiences that he had already completed.

SOUL EXPLORATIONS

WHO GREETS US WHEN WE LEAVE OUR PHYSICAL BODIES?

When we leave our physical body, we are not alone, although at first we may feel as though we are. If this is the case, in our thoughts we can ask for inner help. This brings other Spirit Beings closer to us. If we have some emotional attachments, perhaps to a loved one who has already passed over before us, then it is natural that we have a longing for that soul to be there for us. Because of this, the souls we love and know from our physical life could well be the ones we encounter first. When we do meet them, we feel great joy and the fulfilment of a profound reunion. It is possible that other souls are also there who are important for us to meet.

Going to the Spiritual World after death is a transition process. Those who have faith proceed with confidence and immediately move to the Light. However, not everyone is ready when they die. Some are very confused and might not know what to do or where to go and may not want to accept what has happened to them. Rather than going to the Spiritual World where their perception can expand with Light and love, some souls may decide to stay isolated. They may weave a pattern of reality around themselves, which is more what they want to believe rather than being true. Sooner or later, these created realities will no longer satisfy the soul, who will feel the longing to return home to the Spiritual World where they belong. However, sooner or later, those souls are likely to ask questions and sense that knowing inside of them that they need to go home.

We all have a Spirit Guide, Angel, or teacher who will be waiting for us when we die. Meeting our Guide will be a great source of inner comfort. Guides are there to support us spiritually, and to help us grow on our path. When souls mature, they may have less need of their Guide. They will know what they need to do. But for most souls, especially when they have been through a traumatic time on Earth, they will need their Guide's immense support. They may need counselling and to process emotions. Souls may not be ready to have substantial contact with loved ones until they have been through this cleansing process to find peace and understanding. This will be a first step when a soul comes into the Spiritual World, so that their perception can be clear.

When people first become aware of other souls in the Spiritual World while undergoing a regression session, these other souls can appear like Light Beings. Without our physical bodies, we are beings of Light, and we perceive others that way too. In our soul consciousness, we still have thoughts and feelings. Our perceptions can be deeply passionate and with much greater understanding than we had when in our physical body. We communicate telepathically.

The members of our physical family that we meet when we die could be souls that we also know very well in the Spiritual World; they could be companions with whom we travel for many, many of our lifetimes. Meeting them will be so natural. However, it is also possible that when we reach the Spiritual World, we find that the connection that we share with those souls who were our family members is not so strong. Instead, we could find that there are other souls that we know in the Spiritual World much better than the ones we knew as our family in the preceding lifetime. We may find we have a spiritual family that is different to the family we had while in a physical body.

It is interesting the families that we choose to be born into. Perhaps we were choosing a life where we could become much stronger in our own sense of identity rather than relying and leaning upon those other souls whom we know best. We may have been seeking a life where we could assert our own individuality. Alternatively, we may feel that we need the support of souls we love dearly to be near us. Another possibility could be that we know some souls in the life that we have entered but not others. There can be many reasons. It may be that our soul wants to learn greater compassion to love others and being born with other souls whom we hardly know give us a chance to express this.

If we are a developed soul, we may not need a soul family or soul group so much. We could be adept at shining our own Light. Our focus could be more with helping others and being of service. We may come to Earth for that reason, to assist others and grow through expressing unconditional love. There may be souls around us who are less developed, and we could be teaching those souls by being a model to them so they can learn lessons.

Sometimes we meet souls to share love with them, and other times they could present big challenges, perhaps give us a soul lesson by creating a situation that is difficult for us. In terms of our soul growth, it is important for us to express as much integrity in our life with other people as we can.

The souls we meet in the Spiritual World after our past life death can therefore be there for many reasons. We need to be open, to discover what those reasons are.

SOUL COMPANIONS

As we travel through incarnations from one life to another, we meet many other souls who we know from our home in the Spiritual World.

In our regression state, we may sense it when we meet a soul that we already know. It could come to us as a knowing or feeling of inner recognition. There may be many kinds of relationships that we share with other souls. With souls whom we deeply love, we may be with them to help each other to grow, to provide love and support so that the time on Earth can be easier. We may link with souls who are more advanced than we are who teach and help us in some way. On Earth, we may not recognise them for who they are, and they may not be consciously aware of it either, but, deep inside, the truth of our soul relationships is evident.

We may also mingle with souls who are less developed than us. It may be our inner task to help them, and to support them through their mistakes and their journey to become more mature. That does not mean that we need to be perfect around them. But they may be inclined to have a more limited outlook or be a bit all over the place, more than us. From one life to another, our soul relationships with others change form. Our relationships experience continual evolution and exploration as we reach out for new learning to help us grow.

There are some souls we meet who we are associated with for the duration of our lives, while others the contact may be brief. The souls we know very well in Spirit, even if our meeting with them is brief, still affect us somehow. When we meet with a more advanced soul, we feel the depth of their being and sense there is more to them than what is on the surface. With every soul, there is a purpose for our meeting, even with those whom we are meeting for the first time. Meeting souls we have not met before is a test for our openness. There are aspects in the characteristics of every soul we meet that can help us on our path towards further growth.

Our soul desire is to reach out. How we deal with that is up to us.

ANCIENT CIVILISATIONS

We learn a lot about history when we access past lives. If we take notice of the clothing, architecture of buildings, housing and utensils, race, and culture of the lifetime we access, then we can gain quite an accurate sense of a historical period. Some clients have undertaken considerable research to ascertain that what they experienced can be verified by history books and academic findings. This is not always so easy to do. Some past life memories lack specific information that can place or date the past life. For instance, the lifetime we enter may be one situated in the countryside away from civilisation. It could be set in a village with truly little to distinguish it from hundreds of other villages that could have existed over centuries of time.

What is interesting, though, is that people can have regressions that go so far back in time it is suggestive of civilisations on Earth that have not been confirmed to exist by scholars. Some of these experiences are of mythological or legendary places that have been speculated about. Others are of unknown origins. Such regressions can be fascinating, full of emotion and vibrant experiences, quite believable with the intensity with which they are expressed.

Many people who have worked with me have been attracted to ancient Egypt, wondering if they have had past lives there. Some are attracted to the thought that they may have once been a high priestess or priest working in an illustrious temple. Others sense a strong identification with some powerful pharaoh. However, most of the past life experiences I have witnessed from ancient Egypt have not been like this.

What my clients have shown me about the culture of ancient Egypt is a society that was corrupt and cruel, with many slaves and much poverty. Even the priesthood seems to have been filled with corruption. Except on rare occasions, it does not seem to have been a very pleasant place to be.

There have been people whose regressions to Egypt have suggested that they lived there in an earlier time prior to recorded history. There have been indications of pyramids and even the Sphinx having been built in this earlier period. What has been notable is that in these earlier times, there was much more water. The landscape was not nearly as desert-like as it became later. At this time, the society seemed somewhat gentler than the later times. There was still corruption and power struggles, but not to the same extent. Some of the more interesting regressions relating to this earlier Egyptian period give indications of advanced beings who had come from other worlds. These beings seem to have been living among the local human population in Egypt. Some clients have accessed early Egyptian lives where they were communicated with beings from other worlds. Perhaps, some of the advanced nature of the civilisation in Egypt could have been due to extraterrestrial help.

The impression I have with collating information from various clients is that this earlier civilisation went through a fall at some stage, for reasons which are not clear. Then gradually, from the scattered remnants that remained, the people resurrected elements of the culture into the Egyptian civilisation that we are familiar with today.

Another ancient civilisation that has attracted much attention through regression has been memories relating to the mythical land of Atlantis. Numerous clients have accessed experiences of lives that they have identified as being on Atlantis. Not all of these have been consistent, and some could have been from other ancient societies upon the Earth which have been lost.

Twenty years ago, I wrote a book called *Atlantis the Dark Continent* which was based upon regressions relating to the civilisation of Atlantis. According to the regressions, Atlantis did exist as a rather large continent in the Atlantic Ocean. It was a volcanic land with high mountains and abundant crystalline structures that opened people's psychic abilities. The people of Atlantis were very much attuned to the Spirit of the Earth. People were seduced by the love of power with the psychic energy available. This was misused, culminating in the eventual destruction of the land. I remember with my last regression upon Atlantis the enormous sadness that I felt about the devastation of that land. I did not understand how people could allow a resource so precious to be destroyed.

Another civilisation from before Atlantis existed attached to part of what is now South America, on the Pacific Ocean side. In this land, there was infiltration from people coming from other worlds. It seemed to be another place where people became obsessed with power. People built these enormous towers and became involved in forms of wizardry and use of psychic power to control others. Gradually, these power-seeking people drained the land of life energy until it slowly subsided and much of it went into the sea. It appears as a quite different way of life to what we are used to today, a bit like a Harry Potter type of world. Sometimes, the civilisation is referred to as 'Lemuria'. I have had some regressions where I sensed myself to be living there. Doing these regressions, I could feel that my soul was less mature and less layered than it is today. There were many lessons then about the use of power, but in a different way from Atlantis.

Some other fascinating regressions have been with clients who lived human-like lives in a swampy land with a humid climate at the time of dinosaurs and other giant reptiles. I have not come across many of these, but my sense is that the Earth was seeded with people from another world who arrived in some form of spacecraft. These people lived in colonies for a considerable duration and lost contact with their home world. They seemed to be relatively peaceful souls. Certainly, they needed to be skilful to survive in the environment that existed then. Eventually, they died out, for reasons that I do not know. In my opinion, there was no linage that continued from the human-like beings who existed then to the modern Homo sapiens who we are today.

From other isolated regression sessions that I have witnessed and been through myself, I believe that there were other advanced ancient civilisations that existed on Earth. Included was a civilisation called 'Mu' that flourished in a vast landmass in what is now the Pacific Ocean. Another powerful society that existed in remote times appears to have been settled in what is now the Siberian region of Russia. There could have been a settlement in the region we now know as Antarctica, and one that was in the northern Norse regions at a time when the land structures were quite different from what they are now.

There are many more locations than what I've listed. The impression I have from all these regressions is that our Earth was seeded with human-type beings that came from other worlds. Not all these humanoids adapted well to living on our planet, and some had their own agenda. There were Indigenous humans who adjusted well and loved the Earth and lived in a state of harmony with it. Some of those coming from other worlds came here to use the resources that Earth provided for their own gain and comfort.

It appears that all these ancient civilisations have risen and fallen as others from our known history have done. Generally, they have left little or no traces behind them and it is hard to date them. Some of them could originate from times at least tens of thousands of years ago, perhaps even longer. The regressions I have witnessed have given indications of wars, Earth changes and difficult weather conditions as possible reasons that these ancient civilisations met their demise.

The existence of these places is speculative. Without any historical records to back up what people have experienced in their consciousness, then the reality of these civilisations is completely unproven. Not that many souls who live upon the Earth today are so old to have lived human lives at these ancient times. Even with old souls that I do come across in my work, these ancient lives from far distant ancient civilisations are seldom relevant to my client's lives today. It is interesting to research though.

FUTURE LIVES

Future life exploration is an aspect of spiritual research that can yield fascinating results. In our consciousness, we have maps of possible future lives. As humans we have freewill, therefore we cannot be certain of the future. We have some events that are fated in our lives. However, even fated events can happen in a variety of ways. These all depend on how we respond to situations as they present themselves.

For instance, when we are in the Spiritual World making plans for our forthcoming lifetime on Earth, we may plan to meet with another soul at a certain juncture in our lifetime. The plan could give us the opportunity to form a relationship with this other person and spend the rest of our lives with them. Numerous outcomes could then occur. We might meet that person and form a lifelong relationship as planned. Or, perhaps on that day we were scheduled to meet, we might have had an argument with someone at work, be distracted and miss all the signals and fail to meet this person. Perhaps we may not have adequately dealt with all the steps in our lives leading up to this meeting. We may not have disentangled ourselves from our parents sufficiently for instance. Our parents might have very fixed ideas about who would be an acceptable partner for us and who would not be. Then when we meet this person, even though we may love them, we might decide that we cannot live with them because they do not fit the criteria of an acceptable partner, as outlined by our parents, so we are not receptive to our heart's desires.

There could be many other possibilities as well. Even though our soul and Spirit may encourage us to do what has been planned, if we are not receptive or open enough within the opportunity could be lost. In this case, our lives may go in an entirely different direction to what we had planned. This shows us that what is planned and foreseen for our lifetime may turn out vastly at variance with what our soul has anticipated. This is how the future exists more in the realm of possibilities and probabilities rather than certainties.

Future life projections can tell us what kind of situations our soul may want us to go into for our inner learning and unfoldment. They can give insight into our potential and speculate about the way our world could be in the future. However, this may not be accurate in terms of the way things turn out.

Let me give an example of how future lifetime progressions can be therapeutically useful. One of my client's went through a series of regressions concerning lifetimes where he had closed his heart and been cruel and indifferent to other people. These lives were not very pleasant for my client to go through. The pattern of having his heart closed repeated itself many times in various lifetimes. However, he felt for his own peace, that he had to go through these lives. Gradually, he was learning of the need for him to love himself. Each of these closed lives helped him to feel a little lighter and more able to accept himself. As he accessed past lifetimes closer to present time, he found that he was doing better at keeping his heart open. It was clear that he was gradually learning his lesson as a soul. This was helping him also with relationships he was experiencing in his present life. At one point, I suggested that he do a future lifetime with me. When he went into this, he found himself living in a community setting. His heart was open. He was treating those around him with love, kindness, and respect. He loved nature, lived simply and basically had a very fulfilling life. Others regarded him well. It seemed that all the deficiencies that he had suffered in his past lives were now overcome. My client was exceedingly happy. Whether or not this future lifetime would ever take place as he envisioned it didn't matter – what it showed him was a direction forward. He could conceive that he was on the right track. Continuing to make improvements with his behaviour in the way that he was doing would have their rewards. The future was bright. My client was very satisfied. That was the last session we did together.

Looking at future lives may not benefit everyone, but for some it can give an assurance they are on the right soul path.

REGRESSION CONCEPTS

THE EVOLUTION OF THE SOUL

One of the mysteries of existence is our beginnings. There is a vast universe around us. Within that, we express our own unique individual consciousness that is called our soul. How is our soul formed, and what is our potential? My speculation is that we are formed from some spark of God or Source, and that our potential is for us to embrace consciously all that we are in terms of that being of God. The force or impulse that has brought us into being is essentially love. At the core of our consciousness, we know that we are connected lovingly with all other beings. We are distinctive, and continually evolving. We strive to reach a state of consciousness of oneness and unity with our Divine self. There are many stages on this journey. One stage we can go through is for us to incarnate in human lifetimes upon the Earth.

Our soul is pure energy, and consciously exists in spiritual dimensions that we cannot fully perceive during our physical existence. The Spiritual World, where we feel at home, exists in a higher vibration than what we experience upon the physical Earth. Here, there is much love and beauty. We feel a great connection with all fellow beings that are with us. When we can embrace our awareness in the Spiritual World, we have a much vaster perspective about all forms of life than we do when we are on the Earth. By experiencing our consciousness in the Spiritual World, our perception, wisdom, and ability to engage with love is magnified to a great degree compared to our capabilities to do so as humans. When we are in the Spiritual World, we can express ourselves much more fully and we feel connected with whom we really are. Our soul is multidimensional. While some aspects of our soul can incarnate upon the Earth, our Higher Self essence remains in the Spiritual World.

When we incarnate on Earth, some aspect of our soul constricts itself to adapt to the lower vibration of physical life. We go through a process in the womb, of combining our soul energy with the DNA of the physical foetus. The physical body becomes a secondary home for our soul while we consciously go through a human lifetime on the Earth. The mother and father that we choose are related to us through the physical DNA of our foetus.

It is uncomfortable for us to be physically incarnated. Usually in the Spiritual World, we experience much more space, freedom, and awareness. We miss that coming to Earth. Our perception is restricted by the physical body we inhabit. We may have dispositions brought about by the DNA of the foetus we inhabit. It is our challenge and task to determine what we do with those tendencies and inclinations. When we are in the Spiritual World, we are so accustomed to the feeling of oneness with all life that we never feel alone. In the low vibration of physical existence, we do not feel that oneness nearly as easily. Instead, we feel separation and loneliness, and we have a great longing for love, and to feel more connected.

For our soul to experience such spiritual separation is exceedingly difficult. We want to find that feeling of love and connection with which we are so familiar and have to work extremely hard to attain it. There is a connection with our Higher Self that continues to function, and we have to strive to open it. In some incarnations, the connection to our Higher Self may be strong by virtue of the DNA we have inherited, and in other incarnations it could be weak. The more that we can strengthen that inner connection, the easier it is for us to fulfil our life purpose.

Our soul purpose can have many aspects to it, or it could

be quite simple and specific. Each physical lifetime we seek to make some steps towards gaining inner knowledge and expressing love. We have challenges to meet, so we can stand on our own feet, and find our strength sufficiently. It helps us when we can channel spiritual energies through us, to raise our vibration and the vibrations of life around us. For developed souls, it is like we are working to bring the Spiritual World onto Earth. As human beings, we tend to make lots of mistakes. There can be many pitfalls where we can falter in our development. We do not always succeed in our purpose.

We go through life using our freewill. It is up to us to make our own decisions. If we make decisions and confine ourselves to doing only what others tell us to do, then we do not learn very much. If we do not have a spiritual outlook, our reaction to life may be largely instinctive. Then the impulses of behaviour coming from our DNA governs our behaviour. If we listen to our hearts and intuition, then we learn more and be likely to act more truly in accordance with our purpose. As we can open our hearts and feel how our heart wishes to love, then we open our connection with our Higher Self. We can listen to our conscience, which tells us what feels right and wrong. Our intuition is like an inner voice or prompting that supports us to make steps in our life that draws us closer to our inner truth.

When we consider the life that we have lived, it becomes clear how we have fared. The purpose and learning may be quite different from what we had supposed, and in understanding this there is a feeling of recognition. We may become aware of some inner tasks with which we have succeeded in that life and feel joy, or if we have made mistakes and missed opportunities, we feel disappointed. However, the chance will be there for us to try that lesson again in another life. All is not lost. This is all part of the learning for us, as we go through the regression experience. What we will realise is that we are on a growing evolving path, and this is what we deeply want to do.

GENETIC MEMORY AND CELLULAR MEMORY

When we incarnate to a life on Earth, our soul joins with the foetus to form a conscious growing human organism. The foetus contains the DNA from both parents, and the combination of this DNA generates physical traits, behaviour dispositions and even psychic imprints from our ancestors. This provides a grounding of how our life is formed. The outer layers of our consciousness largely enact the programming that our DNA gives us. This includes our instinct which exists as a herd-like sense of belonging with our family and the culture and society around us. We feel a fundamental urge to ensure our survival and to fight or flee from danger. Our soul is independent of all this. Because our soul comes from a spiritual Source of love, there is no compulsion within our soul to follow genetic programming. Because our soul is residing within our physical body it is not be able to ignore the genetic programming that is present.

Our soul situates itself most strongly in our heart. In our heart we feel love and connection, and this extends to an awareness of Spirit. Our soul is not physical in nature, but energetic. As we grow, the soul calls on us to connect with it. In the outer realms of our awareness as a human being, there is a shell-like structure of our consciousness which we could call our ego. The ego drives forward our actions and reactions in life, and it assumes elements of control over what we do. Until our soul can break through this shell, then our ego holds sway over how we react, and we live our lives more in a mode of automatic pilot. When we awaken to it, our inner knowing consciously influences the way we live our life. Our soul has its own reasons for joining with the genetic imprints of the foetus, and it is eager to break through the shell of the ego to direct our life towards more worthwhile channels.

It could be, for instance, that our physical body has inherited behavioural predispositions towards being violent and antisocial. These tendencies may have expressed themselves in several of our ancestors. It now exists in the cellular memory of our identity. While the soul is not able to eradicate the genetic tendencies, it may be able to transform those traits if it can assert itself. The soul may influence the genetic predisposition towards violence by transforming it into the fight for justice or human rights. The soul can bring love and wisdom into genetic trends so that those traits become much more constructive and worthwhile.

The soul seeks to bring about transformation and healing to the genetic make-up of our physical body. When our soul can influence our ego, then it brings with it a higher vibration of responses to our life. The cellular structures of experience within the physical body are changed through this and ultimately transformed. The genetic patterning of our body is affected by the presence of our soul. As our soul asserts itself, this can bring about healing – not only for us, but for the generations to follow as well.

If the soul is not able to break through the ego shell in a lifetime, then, from a soul perspective, that lifetime is largely wasted. The experience within that body has followed the programming set by the DNA structure without self-reflection or evolution. Sometimes, the human body that we choose, contains DNA that our soul can use positively and easily to achieve its goals. On other occasions, the DNA of the body contains a lot of challenges that need to be worked through. The DNA within the body is what we need to confront as souls for us to learn our inner lessons.

For instance, when we are born, we may carry genetic tendencies towards general addictive behaviour. For our soul to work through this we need a lot of love and strength from Spirit. Our body will need to learn self-love so that we can care for our body and nurture its existence. By doing this we may have a worthwhile life of compassion, and perhaps serving others. If our soul remains suppressed, we may well succumb to addictions and eventually die without any resolution.

THE PROCESS OF REBIRTH

The period before we die can be quite intense. With our attachment to the physical body, approaching death is a great step into the unknown. Our ego generally loosens its hold over us just before we die. This enables our soul awareness to express itself more fully. The moments leading to death may be peaceful or a struggle, depending upon what is going on for us. However, the moment of passing when we take our last breath, is characterised by a significant transformation. Our soul leaves the physical body and suddenly we feel free. We may be next to the body or above it, or else we could rise rapidly upwards. There are various possibilities. We could feel lingering emotion about what happened at the end of that life, or we might feel relief and be ready to go on. Some souls are concerned about those they have left behind and want to stay to support them and watch over them. If the death were traumatic, the shock of that could mean that we need to come to terms with that before we can move on. If we experienced guilt about how we lived our life we may be afraid of meeting God, or we may feel angry if we have felt life has been unjust.

As we approach the Light, we combine once more with our Higher Self, and our soul feels more united with a greater perspective of who we are. Even for those souls who remain close to the physical plane after the moment of passing, eventually, the urge to return home directs them upwards to the Light. Some souls may not want to admit the truth of how they lived their lives, but eventually, there is a calling to return to our spiritual home.

When we reach the Light, it is an experience of truth, and there can be no escaping from the fruits of all our activities. The outcome of the life review may be happy for us or a disappointment. We may be surprised to perceive that we learned more than we thought we had. From the human perspective, we might have felt that we were successful in some ways but not in others, but all this may be different as we go through the review process. A moment of kindness and opening of our heart may be of more significance than many other achievements that we thought were worthwhile.

The result of the life review helps determine what our next steps and how we can move forward best in the further evolution of our soul. We may need to plan for another lifetime on Earth, perhaps to seek out some additional learning for limiting patterns that we were working on in the lifetime we have just finished. There may be themes from other lifetimes we have had where we need to develop our awareness and abilities to manage various situations we would encounter. Otherwise, we could be ready for some new learning with themes that test us in ways that we have not encountered before.

From my work with clients as a Life Between Lives® Therapist, working with the method of Dr Michael Newton, I have been astonished at how multifaceted the Spiritual World can be. The more that we develop as souls, the more choice we have about what we choose to do. We take on more responsibility and become more skilful in terms of our energetic actions. There are mental worlds we can visit and higher realms in terms of energetic vibration. We can gain spiritual learning with souls more learned than us. We can also engage with healing and helping with young souls who are needing to grow, on Earth and other places. All these experiences offer their own challenges and opportunities.

At some point we reach a stage where there is no need for us to incarnate upon physical worlds. For those souls who are mature and developed, this process is voluntary. When we are less developed, it is necessary to remain on the wheel of physical existence, and this continues until we have learnt enough as souls so that we can move on. Some souls are enthusiastic and welcome further physical incarnations, others feel resistant and wish that they did not need to do it. However, the experiences on Earth, and the challenges that we put ourselves through while we are here offer the necessary learning that helps us to grow stronger and more robust as souls.

Our Guides and spiritual teachers help us prepare for an incarnation. The more developed we are, the more we can do much of the preparation work on our own. For our coming physical incarnation, we not only have to take account of our own experiences, but also other souls with whom we are likely to interact. We have to be mindful of the social and cultural situations which we are likely to encounter. What conditions will best suit what we must learn? For our human minds, it seems like an incredibly complex task to organise. However, in the Spiritual World, it will proceed smoothly.

In this preparation phase, we can make plans about the shape of our life. Sometimes these plans can be very precise, others there may be left a lot left open. The process of entering our physical incarnation is not an easy one. When we die, we experience an expanse of awareness and freedom as we rise to the Light and return home, whereas when we go into physical birth it is the opposite and we go through a contraction of awareness and perspective. Our awareness of the Light and love of Spirit is diminished, but we still need it.

Within our soul, we carry imprints of our plans for our physical life and the lessons that we have set for our self to experience. As we descend to unite into physical form in the foetus, our awareness of this plan is very much reduced. There is a thread of Light from our energy system that links our physical self with our Higher Self. Meditation and inner awareness practices enable us to open the channels to our Higher Self. Doing meditation helps us to tune in to inner stillness and our spiritual purpose.

There are many paths that we can choose to live while on Earth. One pathway we may choose is to live a life of being a healer in service to others. Very often, souls embarking on this pathway choose particularly challenging bodies and parental patterns to be born into. They will need strong resolve to fulfil their intentions. Such souls may feel the need to learn directly about the suffering humans can go through and how to endure this. If they can get through this themselves, then they will be able to help others later, when they are older.

They are likely to be highly sensitive souls, who are greatly affected by others' emotions. If they have chosen parents who are living according to abusive patterns, they have to work out how to survive this emotionally. They also have to overcome the influences of the emotional projections of their parents and culture so that they can be free from this. It is likely that there will be a crisis in the life of this soul. This could be planned to precipitate spiritual searching and a need to discover deeper learning and insight. This juncture in the soul's life is a healing crisis. There may be much emotional, mental, and psychic residue that the soul must release. This process can be difficult and require a great deal of integrity, trust, and commitment to uncover illusions and patterns that are not in tune with their soul.

Eventually, when this soul has uncovered a truer sense of who they are, then they can bring spiritual love and Light into their being. They can renew themselves in a way that more fully reflects their spiritual purpose. When they can do this, they will also be equipped to help others who have also suffered from emotional and mental wounds.

As souls we all have a purpose to find who we truly are, and to express that in all facets of our life. To accomplish this, we need to open our awareness to our Higher Self and the reality of Spirit. We do this through meditation, truth seeking, healing and love. Our greatest healing power is expressed through love. Fear is the biggest challenge we must overcome, and love is the energy that enables us to do that.

THE CHANNEL BETWEEN THE EGO AND SOUL

The ego is the consciousness of our personality, the surface of our consciousness. Our ego makes decisions, forms concepts, and relates to other people; it defines the world around us. Our ego has a natural tendency to seek control and to manipulate what we do in ways that suit us. Our ego speaks of who we are as 'I' and this implies the capacity for self-awareness.

For many people the existence of our ego is the sum and total of who we are, and there is no life after death. Such people come to this conclusion through a belief that they have decided upon. This belief states that we are no more than our physical body, and that what we perceive through our physical body with the aid of our brain is all that we are, our only existence. People who have this outlook do not accept the existence of the soul.

In contrast to this, for those with spiritual faith, our soul does exist and is our individual essence. The soul is not confined to the physical body, and it has a spiritual nature which is eternal. Spirit is an energy that permeates all living beings. Our soul is at one with Spirit which is an expression of oneness. Therefore, in our pure soul state we feel loving connection with all beings and that there is a unity within all life. Our ego may not accept that. It has a limited perspective and does not perceive beyond its own boundaries. For those of us with faith, our ego may have a broader outlook and be willing to accept the possibility of life after death.

When our awareness is confined to our ego, we are concerned with what we want, what we know, and we like the world around us to be predictable. In this state, we do not have a lot of outward perception because of the control patterns that we have constructed. Those control patterns form boundaries of what we are prepared to believe is possible and what is not. Our ego has belief systems that have been constructed by precepts we have agreed upon with expectations that we do not wish to disturb. Whatever might exist beyond those boundaries is likely to be dismissed. The ego exists in part through fear, and it is fear that compels us to contract our awareness causing us to seek an illusion of control and security to feel safe. Our ego is like a shell around us, and it feels fear for all those areas of life where it lacks control.

Our soul is not constrained like the ego. However, when our soul joins with the physical form of the foetus, it sets itself a task of learning to communicate with the ego with the hope that the ego and soul act in harmony. They are both vital aspects of our human existence. Our soul flows with the feelings of our heart while our ego may close our heart and not be willing to recognise our soul for who it is. When we can open our awareness beyond the surface reaches of our consciousness, perhaps through meditation, then this gives our soul the opportunity to express itself. When our awareness opens to the possible existence of soul consciousness and what this entails, then whole new worlds open to our human existence. If our ego accepts this, our inner life can expand, and our ego is less rigid in how it conceives reality. We then no longer function as two separate entities divided but find union and strength of purpose.

There is often struggle at first, when the ego becomes aware that there is the possibility of some greater sense of being beyond what it had cognition previously. Our ego can easily close itself to new possibilities when it feels threatened. However, if what is suggested appears more positive, then it may be willing to consider it. The ego does need to challenge new awareness that may impinge upon its control. It can be helpful for our ego to develop clear thought and a willingness to question what is true and false. If our ego is not willing to do that, then we are in a cage or prison inside our self. Once our soul and the ego can communicate, then it is possible for the ego to experiment so that its awareness can grow and expand one step at a time. Only then, can trust gradually form. From there our ego can come to appreciate the value of faith and allow spiritual unfoldment to take place.

At its best, the ego and our soul can work in partnership. As humans, we need both to be operating with strength and harmony. The thought processes of our ego give context for the experiences we have. Our soul channels love, awareness, and wisdom, allowing us to find a deeper more meaningful purpose in all our actions. It is one of the main purposes of our human existence to encourage our soul and ego to combine. This is also relevant to past life regression. Our soul channels memories of other lives that we have lived. Our ego may not fully understand what these past lives mean and where they come from. However, if our ego can accept the experiences then the meanings and spiritual knowledge inherent in these experiences can work through us and help us grow.

When our ego can absorb experiences of past lives and awareness of the Spiritual World into our being, then this widens our perspective. It enables our energy field to broaden, and once our ego is open to it, then we can channel more spiritual energy into our life on Earth.

One of my long-term clients has had to work out an enormous

personal struggle with his ego. In lifetime after lifetime, his ego has wanted to take over, to be in control. In some of his past lives, his ego sought power to subdue life around him to his will. But the only way he could do that was to use his will to suppress his heart. Consequently, his past lives have often been filled with suffering and unhappiness. In his life this time, he has had similar struggles. But now he has reached a point where he no longer wants to continue this struggle. His wish has been to find peace. Gradually, through many sessions of therapy, he has been able to tame his ego and allow space for his heart to express itself. His heart and ego have begun to cooperate and his faith in Spirit has grown. He has found great fulfilment in his inner work, and it has led to a substantial improvement in his life.

AGE REGRESSION

One of the techniques used by therapists to regress people into past lives is Age Regression. With this process, people can be guided into a hypnotic state to experience memories from times going back further and further into their childhood. By asking detailed questions, the client moves from a state of consciousness and exploring known memories to an awareness where lesser-known memories start to reveal themselves.

While the memories are known, the client may still believe that they have some control over the process. The therapist uses techniques of progressive relaxation to ensure that the client becomes increasingly receptive. At some point, the therapist suggests their client goes to a memory that the client does not normally recall. Then this begins a process where the client knows that they are no longer in control. For some people, to feel that they no longer have control may cause a reaction of panic. But when they are being reassured and feel relaxed, they trust their therapist and accept what is happening. As the client surrenders to the experiences that they are having, then this takes them into a deeper state where there is less resistance to earlier memories coming forward.

Once in this deeper state of inner acceptance, the therapist can ask for the client to recall memories from even earlier in their life. They can go to when they were truly little, being a toddler and even as a baby. The client goes into the awareness of their soul consciousness. They are able to describe their environment, and even their feelings at what is going on. There could be memories when they experience that they were not in their body. Instead, they were watching from above. Some souls take a long while before they settle to being in their body more permanently. They may continue to come in and out of the body long after birth. It can be interesting for the client to experience such memories and other memories from their early life. Many of these recollections can usually be verified by family members afterwards.

In this deep state, the client may be able to recall the time of being physically born. Going through the memory of their actual birth can be full of feelings and energetic sensations. The client experiences the tension prior to the birth and the release once their body has emerged from the womb. They may also be aware of the emotions of those round them. There can sometimes be trauma residues from this time that need therapy.

From there, the therapist can guide the client back further and ask about their experiences in the womb. Not all people have strong memories from this period. The client may not have been so consciously present while their body was in the womb. The body will have been going through its natural physical growing process. The soul may not have been in the body at the time. For those who were present in the womb, they may sense their mother's heartbeat, thoughts, and emotions. They are certainly aware of the physical aspects of what was going on. From the late stages in the pregnancy, they may recall feeling quite squashed and uncomfortable. When they access memories from early in the pregnancy, they feel that they have plenty of room and able to move about easily.

From these beginning stages of connection with the physical body of the foetus, the client may become aware of thoughts and feelings they had then about their mother, their father, and even other people. The client can also be guided to a time before they join the physical body. At this time, they are channelling directly the memories of their soul.

It is possible that the soul could have felt content with the prospects of another human life. Otherwise, the soul may have felt uneasy about what that life would be like. It may have been nervous about the trials that would need to be confronted. If these feelings prevail, the soul could react by being resistant to fully joining with the physical body.

There can be much to be discovered from exploration of the consciousness that we had while in our mother's womb, and even the time before then. Some of this can usually be verified through conversations with our parents or other people who were around during the pregnancy. Obtaining these confirmations can help validate our ability to access far memory from periods of our existence when we would be expected to carry little conscious memory if any.

Once the therapist has done enough exploration from their client's present life, they can ask their client to go back further. That is when past life recall can begin. A simple suggestion like this generally initiates memories from a past life. At this point, the therapist could also make the direct suggestion that the client is now in an earlier time when they had another body. Then they can ask their client to describe where they are and what is happening. This is sufficient to begin a past life regression exploration.

EXPLORING PAST LIVES

CAN ANYONE BE A PAST LIFE REGRESSION THERAPIST?

Sometimes people feel it is enough to learn regression by watching a video on YouTube or by reading a script detailing a past life regression. For some people, that could be sufficient to allow some memories and experiences from a past life to come into awareness. The memories that come forward may be quite dramatic and emotional, or quite ordinary and nondescript. This could show that past life experiences do exist.

If you want to learn in depth about past lives, or become a past life therapist, there is much to learn. The skills needed to navigate someone through one of their past lives to enable that person to experience healing and spiritual insight are considerable. To become a proficient past life therapist, much training and experience is needed.

When I first studied hypnotherapy to practise regression on others, I learnt the mechanical processes to lead a person through the main steps of a regression, but there was so much more to learn. The whole experience of regression deals with spiritual realities and the realm of the soul. What does it take for someone to assume that they can guide another person responsibly through the subtle reaches of these realities with the intuitive understanding and awareness that they need? It is not a toy or a game, but a sacred process that impinges directly upon the meaning and purpose of people's lives. Therefore, for someone to do a weekend online course or some technical instruction over a few weeks is very unlikely to provide the skills for a person to support another adequately with regression.

Past life regression work is a sacred endeavour that needs

a great deal of respect. Therapists doing this work are dealing with people's souls: helping them to grow and unfold, overcome problems and to heal. Before I underwent a training in regression, I had done a great deal of research into spiritual science and reincarnation, and I felt that I had a reasonable intuitive understanding of how regression could work. It felt familiar to me, and I felt an excitement learning it. I feel that it has been my vocation to do this work. After my initial training, I did not feel prepared to adequately do the work and I had to go through a lot of trial and error to learn. It was a specialised craft, and for the first few years when I dared to practise it, I knew that I could do better. I felt much better qualified after three years of in-depth training in past life therapy with Dr Roger Woolger. This helped me a lot, but there was still more that I had to learn.

The inner consciousness of people is vastly mysterious. There has never been any stage when I have felt that I could assume that I knew everything that was needed. At times, I have had to call on Spirit to help me. I could not rely upon what I had been taught to give me all the answers. Sometimes, I would need to sit in the silence while connecting with my client, until I would sense the inner guidance of what I needed to do next. As I followed this, it would inevitably work and help me to support my client to go further. It could be such an involved process and I have felt very humble to be able to do it with people. After over 33 years of doing the work, I feel as though I am still learning and improving in the craft of supporting people through these processes. I would discourage people from treating this work lightly.

In ancient times, people would take years to develop the skills and awareness to be a healer. I feel that to be a past life therapist requires a similar dedication of learning.

CONTRAINDICATIONS FOR DOING PAST LIFE REGRESSION

Mostly, if someone approaches me seeking to have a past life regression experience, I support that and do my best to work with them. There are some circumstances when I hesitate and may refuse to do the therapy.

When someone is suffering from mental illness and has difficulty managing their everyday life, to have a regression experience could destabilise them and they may have difficulty in integrating the experience that is revealed to them. It could be that they do not have the inner tools where they can discern what is from the past and what is now. If they have some anchor to help them process what their consciousness presents to them, they may be able to deal with it. They would need mental tools to help them process what they encounter internally, and they would also need support from those around them. Therefore, I would take great care with such people, and before we began, I would ask them to check with their medical practitioner.

Recently, at a Mind Body Spirit Festival, a young woman approached me at my stall for a regression session. She was sensitive and mentally coherent. My intuition told me to work with her. The session took her to a recent lifetime when she committed suicide to end that life. I went into the process of her past life suicide, and what happened after her suicide when she ascended to the Spiritual World. I approached this step by step in great depth and detail. I emphasised how if a person ends their life prematurely that they are highly likely to have to return and live a similar lifetime again, confronting similar conditions. To commit suicide was not a great thing to do.

The young woman was moved by the session. She shed many tears. I sensed that what she experienced had challenged her outlook of life greatly. At the end of the session, she seemed deeply thoughtful. The session had obviously had a strong resonance with her. My intuition told me that it was possible that she was someone who had had suicidal thoughts or even attempted her own life. I did not know for sure. What I hoped was that the past life would act as a deterrent to her. It was one of those occasions when I had to trust that she was guided to me for a reason. As she walked away from me, I prayed for her and wished her well.

I choose not to do past life regression with people who are under the influence of drugs or alcohol. Doing regression work demands concentration, and it is also important for our inner spiritual faculties have clear access to our mind and energy system. When people have been taking drugs or drinking alcohol, what they perceive is distorted and can often lack coherence. It is very unlikely in such circumstances that a past life regression therapy session will be beneficial, and it will probably be a waste of time for the therapist. It may even unbalance the person while they are under the influence of intoxicants.

When people undergo a past life regression session, the experiences they have are usually delicate and subtle. People feel vulnerable after such a session. To integrate a regression session, people need to consider carefully what has occurred in their consciousness and to be open to what that would mean. For the session to have a positive impact, it is greatly helpful for the person to feel supported and validated with their experience. If the client's loved ones can have sympathy, then this can be immensely helpful.

Typically, as an outcome of a regression session people

feel prompted to question and evaluate aspects and patterns that have been operating in their life. This can be a challenging process. For people to accept the past life as it has revealed itself to them may be a significant step towards the life changes that this person needs. If the person encounters someone who is critical of them or closed, this could have a quite negative impact upon the way that the person appraises their session. If someone else ridicules what they have experienced or rejects it in some other way, then the person who has had the regression may well be inclined to reject the past life experience too.

It is much better, for a person who has had a regression to have someone who gives positive feedback to their feelings. This does not mean that the person then must accept the experience without question. We need to question. That is a healthy process. However, negative criticism from someone else is likely to lead to a biased judgement and a closed heart. It is good if people can write down their experience and reflect on it thoroughly. Then they can form their own opinion and be less affected by what other people might say. A regression experience can open our consciousness in ways we have not felt before. It is important for us to honour that in how we integrate it afterwards.

Sometimes, people seek to book a past life session for somebody else. It may be intended as a kind gesture, but I find that it is important for people to make their own informed decision. Past life exploration is profound work where we connect with our soul. It is a deep, personal meditation and not something to be done because of someone else's whim or desire. Regression is a form of therapy work that can change and transform people's lives. Therefore, if you have been invited to have a regression session, you need to consider carefully and decide for yourself if the timing feels right, and if it is truly an experience that you are ready to have. It is a lovely gift to offer another person, but that person needs to be consulted about it before such a session is finalised.

This is similar for children. There are some children who have a sincere interest in knowing their past lives. I have come across children who are eager to have a past life session. Generally, children are open subjects and become aware of the details of one of their past lives easily. However, this is not something to force upon a child, say, because the parent, relative or friend wants to gain information about that child's past lives for their own benefit.

I am open to working with children. The youngest I have worked with so far is a boy who was eight years old. There are some specialists who do regression work with children who are even younger than this. I find that it is important to explain the process thoroughly to the child first so that they understand it and can decide for themselves. Generally, I also find it important for at least one of the child's parents to be familiar with what the regression process involves. Children who are meant to do regression usually know instinctively that it is right for them and are open to go ahead. However, if the child is unsure then it is best to leave it. When a parent explains about regression to their child, it is good if they can do this plainly, and in a neutral manner, so that the child does not feel influenced or pressured one way or the other.

When I work with children, I ask for the parent or guardian to be present. I try to use more simplistic language than I might use with an adult. As I proceed, I endeavour to be cautious, not to expose the child to an experience that could be too psychologically challenging. I need to use my intuition with this. What may be appropriate for one child may not be right for another, and vice versa.

There have been occasions when I have been surprised by the kinds of experiences that children access without prompting. Children can channel experiences where they are adults or being of a different gender from who they are today. They can be aware of being involved in an adult relationship. It can come quite naturally for them also to experience their death in the past life, and they can easily sense themselves rising away from the body they previously had. Children experience the Light and love of the Spiritual World. This can be emotional and moving for the child. They may also meet with their Spirit Guide and become aware of the love and wisdom that their Guide offers them. The exchanges are less sophisticated than with an adult, but on a feeling level the contact with their Spirit Guide can be a hugely transformative and a helpful inner step for that child to make.

Children also need to heal, grow, and learn inwardly. For a child to become aware of their own soul can be strengthening for their character. My experience of working with children has been positive and profoundly helpful for the children concerned. It may be an experience that the child talks about freely with others, or they may prefer to store it away, privately, until a time when they can address it more openly.

A MEDITATION TO EXPLORE ONE OF YOUR OWN PAST LIVES

To learn about your past lives is quite a sensitive exploration. Do this meditation when you are in a clear space, and it feels right. You could embark on this inner journey from a place of curiosity or because there is some topic that you wish to explore. Hopefully, you will access some impressions and insights to help you. Remember that to go into depth with one of your past lives, it will be most advisable to see a reputable past life therapist to guide you.

Find a quiet and centred space to do this guided meditation. Make a recording of it first so you can listen to it. Sit or lie down comfortably. Be in a room or place where you can be reasonably certain that you will not be disturbed. To begin, have your eyes open and take a few deep breaths.

Allow your eyelids to gradually become heavy and slowly close. Focus on your breathing.

With each breath, allow yourself to breathe out anything that has been occupying you. Breathe in peace and relaxation. Let yourself relax with the gentle rhythm of your breathing. Progressively find yourself drifting into a very relaxed and receptive state. Know that you are safe and protected. As you proceed you can become increasingly open.

Imagine a beautiful golden light flowing through your body. Let it travel right through your body to the base of your feet. Let this light relax you and sensitise you as it continues to move through every cell of your being.

Then allow yourself to go down ten steps. If you cannot see the steps clearly, just sense them as if they are there. Let your senses bring these stairs to life, as if they are alive.

Counting down 1... 2... going deeper and deeper... 3... 4... 5... as you go further down, your consciousness opens more and more... 6... 7... 8... nearly there now... 9... and... 10.

Now you are at the bottom of the stairs. There is a door in front of you. This door is the entrance to one of your past lives. Be aware of the form and shape of this door. Notice what features it has. Then determine if you need to push or pull this door open. If it feels right for you, open the door, and take a few steps forward. Allow yourself to step through into the past life on the other side of the door.

So, you are there now, you are in the past life. Start to orientate to the setting of where you are. Notice the environment around you, and the ground under your feet. Focus on that now. What do you sense that you are standing on? Is it stone, soil, wood, grass? What is it? As you become even more aware of that ground, sense what clothes you have on. Are you wearing a lot of clothes or something light? Are you carrying anything, or wearing something on your head? Feel and sense more details about your body. Are you male or female, child, or adult? This is your past life identity. Feel that this person that you are there is becoming more and more real for you. Allow yourself to channel the thoughts, feelings, and energy that you experience, as if this is you. Let yourself embrace that you are this person.

Be aware of the setting where you are. Are you in a room or some other form of enclosed space, or are you out in the open? Notice if there are any people with you, or are you on your own? With the people who are there, tune into them. What is your relationship with them? Feel and sense that. Let yourself become increasingly aware of details and features of the environment where you are. What is occupying you just now? Let the image of where you have started become a living memory. What happens next? Are you walking, standing, involved in a task?

Allow your awareness of the memories within the past life begin to expand. You are now in the place where you live, your home or whatever you feel is your home there. Be there now. It is one of those occasions when you are having a meal. Notice where you are eating. Do you sit at a table, or on the floor or on a bench? As you eat, are there other people or is it just you? Who are the people living with you in this place? Focus upon each one in turn. Do you feel close to them or more distant? If you are on your own, how does that feel? When you come outside, are living in a township or village or out in the countryside?

Become aware of your everyday activities. Sense yourself engaging in what occupies you most. Do you have duties, work or are you able to do what you like? Go through your day now. Allow more and more details to come to you. What is most meaningful for you? Be in a moment when you are experiencing what feels truly meaningful to you. What is it that you are doing? Focus on that now, and then feel what that is like in your body.

Let us find out more about the story of this lifetime. Be in a significant moment that occurs for you. You are there now. Allow your awareness of this situation become clear to you. Are you alone or with others? Notice your thoughts and feelings. Become increasingly aware of what it is about this moment that is significant. Go through this event and notice all that happens. How do you react to any challenges that are there? Let any feelings come to the surface so that you can bring them out. Go through to the outcome of this event. How are you feeling now? What have you decided?

It is now the key event of this lifetime, the experience where you are most tested. Be at this event and sense the drama of what is going on. What are your thoughts and feelings? There could be a dilemma that you are confronting. If you feel fear for any reason, notice where this is in your body. What is that fear saying to you? How do you respond to it? Now proceed through the event and let yourself experience all the details of what takes place. Be aware of your internal beliefs and how these beliefs shape what you do. Keep going forward until this is all over. Then realise what has become of you, and how this experience has affected you.

Let us go forward to the last day of this lifetime. What are you doing? It is just a moment when you reflect over the life you have lived. How do you feel about it? Has it been worthwhile, or does it feel like the life has been wasted? Your death may be sudden, and even traumatic or it may be peaceful. In these last moments, be aware. Are you standing, sitting, or lying? What are your circumstances? Are there other people with you or not? Tune into your emotions. Then slowly move forward. Open your awareness to the details of what is happening.

Now you take your last breath, and your soul emerges from your body. Notice whether you are next to the body or above it. How does it feel to be out of the body? It is likely you will feel freedom and lightness as you leave this life behind you. It is all over now. You can give thanks for what you have learnt, and even the challenges you faced. It is all in the past now.

As you rise higher, you will find yourself feeling freer and more fully yourself. It is an amazing feeling with so much love. Adjust to the love and Light that is there. You may sense other souls. They could be like Light Beings. Sense who they are, and then take in their love. It is unlikely that you will be alone.

Now it is a moment when you can contemplate. What was that life all about? Your perspective is more open now. There may be lessons for you to learn, or understandings you need. You may even sense some resonance from that past life with your life today. Relax with this and be at peace.

To finish, allow a precious experience to reveal itself to you, an experience that will be healing to you. Breathe in whatever it is that comes to you. Learn all that you need to learn, and take that in.

To bring yourself out of the regression, return to the base of the steps that you went down, and then let yourself climb up those steps, one step at a time, stepping right up to the top step, and then bringing all your usual consciousness into your physical body. Feel your consciousness extend to your fingers and your toes, to all parts of your body. Open your eyes, only when you feel ready.

***

Afterwards, you may continue to have some thoughts and feelings about the past life for some hours or even days. There could be additional information about the details of the past life that will come to you. Write this all down in your journal. This will ground what you have experienced and help you process it.

OPENING TO MEMORIES OF YOUR PAST LIVES

Opening our consciousness to the memories of our past lives is a skill that we can develop. We can use guided meditations or videos to help us. Even without those aids, there are simple techniques like going into a state of meditation and then through an inner door that we can use. The more we practise techniques to access our past lives, the more our ability to do this is likely to increase. We need not worry that we will get stuck in the past life. What we are doing is to channel impressions of memories that exist only in the past. We can learn from these memories and acknowledge them, but then we need to let them go. If there is something that is difficult within the experience, then it is important that we seek help.

What comes forward from past life memories is unpredictable. There could be strong emotional content. To work through deeper and more complex past life processes, we probably need the assistance of a trained and experienced past life therapist to support us.

Our inner consciousness works in a way where if we ask it to do a task then it will do its best to do so. If we ask our inner consciousness, say, to reveal to us a past lifetime where we knew the soul our partner previously, then our consciousness generally responds and present an experience where this occurred. This can be quite a subtle process. The identity of our partner's soul in the past life may not be obvious. It is also possible that we could have known our partner's soul in many lives. They could have had a different relationship with us in the past life that is revealed than what is shared today. For instance, our partner's soul could have been a friend, child, parent or even an enemy in the past life. They may also not be the same sex as how we know them today. In our past life experience, we have to use our intuition and sense the energy in the people in the past life, to know which person our partner's soul could be.

If we hold strong feelings about a particular location on the Earth, we may feel drawn to investigate a past life connection with that place. We may have had some memory flashes relating to this location and are likely to be very curious to explore this further. By asking for our consciousness to help us, this assists the memories to come forward. We can explore this on our own if we wish, but it is also best if we put any ideas that we have about this to one side so we can be open. If we are too fixed on a certain period of history, or a character that we expect to have been, it can inhibit the true memory from revealing itself.

There may be other reasons that propel us to seek an exploration of our past lives. We might have a problem such as something that we are irrationally afraid of. Some examples of this might be a fear of dying, of having a child or of getting close to someone in a relationship. There may be no reason for our fear based on what has taken place for us in our present life. The thought could come to us as to whether the source of our fear comes from a past life. We can ask our inner consciousness to show us, so we know if that is true. Then we can begin an investigation.

When we focus on this in meditation or if we have a therapist to help us and we ask to go to the source of our fear, then impressions of a past life may begin to come to us. For instance, with a fear of dying, we could go into a lifetime where we had a traumatic death, and we were distressed about what happened. A fear of having a child may go back to a past life where we suffered from an emotional death during childbirth, or one where we became separated from our child in some awful way. The fear preventing us from opening ourselves to be vulnerable and close to someone in a relationship may originate from a situation where we lost someone whom we loved very dearly. Our lover could have died or left us for some reason. The hurt of any of these things might have carried forward, and we could have decided that we did not want to experience pain like that again.

Exploring our past lives through meditation on our own can give answers to our queries, especially when we are seeking understanding. From this we may find peace. In the case of seeking the source of fears that have operated within us, this can be more complex. Often there are residual emotions and limiting belief systems that have been acquired within the experience of the past life trauma. These need therapeutic treatment with the assistance of a skilled past life practitioner.

Our consciousness does not always cooperate with what we ask it to do. There have been occasions when I have requested on behalf of my client that they recall a lifetime which was peaceful and harmonious. My client may have expressed reluctance to go into anything that would have been too difficult for them. Their wishes may not be granted. The energy of one of our past lives may be just below the surface of our consciousness and waiting to emerge. Whatever we ask our consciousness, in this case, is likely to not be enough to prevent this more testing memory from coming forward. We just need to deal with it and learn from what the experience of the past life discloses to us.

When doing regression work, we need to be flexible. Even with a particularly challenging lifetime that has lots of releasing to be done there will be a pathway to peace. Because of the unpredictability of what can manifest when we experiment with past life regression, this is another reason I generally recommend that you at least have a trained past life therapist on call who you can contact if needed. You may struggle to integrate all the details of the past life experience on your own. A skilled past life therapist can ask questions for you and hold the space for you to enter experiences more deeply. They can help you to work through issues that are there. It is not easy to be a subject going through a regression experience and to be your own therapist at the same time.

JOURNAL KEEPING

Journaling is a particularly useful practice to engage in when doing past life regression work. Writing your experiences down can assist you to gain understanding of the experience. It helps you to ground it in your present reality. When you write or draw the experiences within you, then you may also find that further aspects of the past life memory are released. This can enable you to have a fuller comprehension of what the past life means to you. Once a past life memory has begun to emerge, it is best for this to be fully processed so you can get on with your life without having thoughts and feelings from the past life interfering.

A past life regression session will stir various layers of our inner consciousness. The memories of the past life might trigger reactions from what we have experienced in our present life. There may be questions stimulated about decisions we have made and how we have chosen to live. It may not be easy for us if we realise that we are repeating some limiting patterns now that we also expressed in our past life. This could disturb us and make us feel like we want to change.

Other past life memories may open possibilities for us that we had not considered before. Writing down our thoughts and feelings can help ground those thoughts so that they can more easily work through our system. If we do not write these things down, they continue to swim about inside us, and it can be more difficult for the past life experiences to settle. Writing down may also allow us to recall additional past life memories from what was initially experienced. It can be helpful to note these in our journals for our own research purposes and for our own self-therapy.

Once I had a client who had attended one of my past life regression weekend workshops. A day or two after the workshop was over this participant contacted me, telling me that she was thinking constantly about the past life experiences that she had had. She could think of nothing else. I counselled her to write her experience down to release these thoughts. A couple of days later, I had another phone call from this woman. Again, she was complaining about how impressions from past life she had experienced kept intruding in her mind. I asked if she had written her experiences in her journal. She told me that she had not, so I urged her to do so. A few days later again, she phoned me once more with the same problem. When I questioned her, it became apparent that she still had not written her experiences in her journal. This time, I was a little more forceful to implore her to write her experience down. After that, I did not hear from her again. Later, I found out that she finally did write her past life experiences down, after our last phone call. As soon as she did so, she found the peace she needed.

INTEGRATION OF PAST LIFE EXPERIENCES

When you have had an in-depth past life regression, afterwards, it may still take a while to integrate the experience while it works through your system, even if you have written about it. The time this takes can vary. Sometimes it can take a few days and sometimes longer. If the issues have been properly dealt with, then the outcome from your regression work means you feel clearer and lighter inside. This is a sign that you have reached a new equilibrium.

It can happen that there are further layers of inner work that need to be done. As one layer is cleared another may rise to the surface. This may manifest as unsettled feelings and thoughts, discomfort in your body energy system, or even flashes of memory that disturb you. What emerges is likely to be subtly different from the first regression you had, but possibly still on the same theme. These indicators could be telling you that there is another past life to explore. If the signs that you feel around this are uncomfortable, then you may feel reluctant to approach this next past life and you might try to ignore the signals of what your body is telling you. However, if you are attentive to your body then these signs are the beginnings of what wants to emerge next. You may go into meditation and focus upon those areas of unsettlement. Then you can let yourself journey into any memory which may be there. This could give you clues and glimpses about what needs to be investigated.

Once you have had a few past life sessions, you become

more sensitive to how your body responds. There may be feelings with your intuition that guide you. Some aspects of what your energy body is presenting to you may be difficult for your consciousness to get to and you need your therapist to help you. The advantage of utilising your therapist is that then you can surrender yourself and let your therapist direct the process. You can go deeper into the issues that are there and allow them to find their way to the surface of your consciousness.

Doing inner work is a continually evolving process. Once you have expressed the willingness to explore and work through your past lives, more experiences may continue to come forward. You will know when you have done enough. The energy to continue will no longer be there. For some people, doing a single regression is sufficient, while for others there may be a need for extensive exploration of many lives. When one issue is dealt with, then there may be a pause of weeks or months before another theme presents itself. It could happen sooner. Each new regression tests you in a different way.

It helps your soul growth to do these regression experiences. Through each regression you gain more insight and self-knowledge about the foundation of your essential being. You are able to experience your identity more broadly as a soul who has lived numerous lives. Your perception no longer focuses entirely upon your personality within the present life that you are living today.

When you are engaged in a personal growth process and choosing regression as a tool to do that, you need to be open to allow that process to unfold organically. There are inner forces working with you, including your Spirit Guides. You also have a wise, loving inner being, your Higher Self, supporting you. These forces want you to heal, to clear the inner layers of your being and to help you unfold spiritually. The process of healing can proceed step by step. From one regression being integrated, there will be a pause before you go onto the next step. It will be like an inbreath and an outbreath. As this unfolding journey flows, it feels quite miraculous. Your inner reality has its own intelligence that you can come to rely upon. You may become very absorbed in your inner processes, but you also need to remember the everyday world that you must live. Make sure that you attend to your everyday life when you are doing regression, for this helps keep you grounded, and this also assists the processes happening within you to be assimilated in your system.

As you do more regression, you become familiar with how your inner self operates. It has its own tracks and patterns that help you. The creativity of the process of regression can be fascinating. The journey propels you into new areas of inner experience that you will not have anticipated. Once you have trust in the process, it can be a great adventure of discovery.

CONNECTIONS WITH PEOPLE FROM PAST LIVES

Perhaps you meet someone who feels like your soulmate or twin flame. There may be others whom you also feel you know from other lives. The connections may not be quite as intense as with your soulmate or twin flame, but they can still be enormously meaningful.

When you meet someone with whom you feel a soul connection, it is natural to want to know about the origins of that inner bond. You may discover a past life where you had a positive meeting with this soul. Finding this can consolidate feelings relating to the specialness of this other person for you. However, what you discover from the past does not necessarily determine how the relationship will unfold in the present lifetime. This time, the challenges of what you need to learn with that other soul could be quite different from what you had to learn in the past.

You might have an uneasy relationship with somebody. When you seek regression to get to the source of those feelings, you might find that there was a lifetime where there was some suffering and hurt connected with this other soul. You could have been the perpetrator of that hurt, or the victim. In this lifetime you may need to find forgiveness for this soul so you can both find peace and move on.

Often, we have soul lessons to learn with the various people who pass through our life. The inner reason for meeting them can be quite specific or it can be complex. We sometimes feel an encounter with another person has an inner importance that needs our best care and attention.

We need to be discerning and responsible when we conduct past life regression research, and in the area of past relationships this is no different. Perhaps we might have someone in our life who we feel has wronged us. If we feel angry about this when we do regression in relation to this person, we could easily attract a past lifetime where that soul hurt us. This backs up our belief that this soul has been continually cruel to us, and that they deserve some form of punishment. We might decide that we must be better than them in some way. This is our ego seeking information. The lifetime we discover could well be true. However, this could be just one of numerable lifetimes we have shared with that soul.

There could be many other lifetimes where we have been the ones doing the hurting and our soul has wronged them. These lives casting us in a darker light remain hidden until we become open to experience what is true without precondition. The lesson for us in the present life may be about learning to accept this other soul and to forgive what they have done to us. When we rely only on one lifetime we have observed where they have expressed cruelty to us, then we might hold the prejudice that they are the one who owes us. We might carry an aura of self-righteousness around with us, an attitude that is quite unjustified. As with other areas of our life, we can find experiences to confirm our prejudices if that is what we want to find. To seek truth, we need to be willing to confront even the more disturbing areas of our being. This can be deeply challenging, but ultimately more rewarding.

We may meet someone we have strong feelings for that we cannot explain. When we do regression to seek the source of these feelings, we may learn that this soul was our lover in our past life. When we channel such experiences, this can elicit intense feelings of love and desire that existed in the past lifetime. In the present life, this other person may be married or otherwise unavailable. What are we going to do with these feelings? We need to realise what we experienced in the past belongs in the past, and when it comes up, we are being asked to let go.

At first, when we encounter these past life links, it may affect us a lot and even leave us confused. With this kind of experience, we may need to write extensively in our journal. Such an experience raises important questions for us about our relationships now. It is necessary for us to appreciate the deeply passionate feelings we shared with that soul in the past. But we need to honour our present life. Our lesson and reason for meeting this time could be quite different and it is appropriate for us to ask inwardly what the reasons could be. When we begin to sense the truth of how we need to express our connection this time, then the feelings we share with that other person become much quieter. We are able to find peace with that person.

Our family may present us with soul challenges. For example, we could have two children. One of them may feel like a soul that is immensely close to us, while the other soul is feels like one that we hardly know. As a parent, we still need to love both our children. How do we do that? We have to work out how to love unconditionally, and not to favour one over the other. There can be many, varying soul patterns that can come into play within a family. Each pattern has its own lessons and opportunities for growth.

OPPORTUNITIES FOR FURTHER DEVELOPMENT

TRAINING TO BE A PAST LIFE THERAPIST

For those of you interested in training to become a past life therapist, I recommend you first study thoroughly what is available. Past life work is a lot more than reading scripts. You need to gain a detailed experiential understanding of what can occur in a session and how you would deal with it. Training to learn to be a capable and sensitive past life therapist is something that will take considerable time and dedication.

I facilitate Past Life Group Workshops where you can both experience your own past life experiences and witness the experiences of others and how I would work with that. However, at this stage, I am not offering full training courses to become a qualified therapist. What I am willing to do is offer my services as a mentor in conjunction with other training that you may be doing. By doing this, I can offer my support and considerable experience to help you.

BOOKING A SESSION WITH PAUL

I offer personal individual sessions of Past Life Regression, Inner Child Healing and Life Between Lives® Therapy. These past life sessions can last one or two hours. One hour is sufficient to gain a thorough exploration of a past life and to journey to the Spiritual World afterwards. Two hours allows more depth and may include the journey to meet your Spirit Guide.

It is also possible to book a half-day or full-day individual retreat. Past Life sessions can be done for therapeutic reasons or as a tool for inner exploration. Inner Child Healing sessions can help you clear and release problems relating to your childhood. The aim of Inner Child Healing is to enable you to feel greater integration with your child self, and to support your child self to feel more loved. Life Between Lives® sessions are specialised sessions designed by the Newton Institute. They usually last four hours. It is advised that you will have undergone at least one session of past life regression prior to doing this profound therapy. The intention of having a session of Life Between Lives® Therapy is to help you open to a direct connection with your soul. By doing Life Between Lives® Therapy, you will learn by experiencing about your place in the Spiritual World. You may meet with your Spirit Guides, soul group and other resources that can enable you to feel increased inner connection. Life Between Lives® Therapy is an excellent tool to help you to gain deep clarity about your inner purpose in living your life now.

For booking any of these sessions, you can contact me via my website: www.soulhypnotherapy.com, or through the Soul Pathways website: www.soulpathways.net. Paul travels a lot with his work. He is happy for you to meet him for a face-to-face session wherever possible. In addition, Paul regularly does individual sessions online, using both Zoom and Skype.

In addition to individual sessions, online workshops on themes related to group past life regression and many other inner development topics are available. These workshops are conducted through Soul Pathways, a working partnership between me and Dee Gutierrez. Day-long and weekend workshops about regression and other related themes are also offered. Find us on Facebook: www.facebook.com/soulpathways.

I am also a regular attendee of Mind Body Spirit Festivals throughout Australia. In these festivals, 20-minute introductory sessions to past life regression are offered. These are quite excellent ways for people to gain an initial experience of past life regressions, and they are immensely popular. These sessions at Mind Body Spirit Festivals are often booked out.

PAUL'S OTHER PUBLICATIONS

Williamson, P 1999, *Healing Journeys,* Capall Bann Publishing *

Williamson, P; Braithwaite, L 2000, *Atlantis: the Dark Continent,* Capall Bann Publishing *

Williamson, P 2003, *Soul Pathways,* Capall Bann Publishing *

Williamson, P 2005, *A Seeker's Guide to Past Lives,* Capall Bann Publishing *

Williamson, P 2008, *Marjorie,* Soul Light Publishing

Williamson, P 2014, *Ilsa: Ancient Celtic Leader,* Balboa Press

Williamson, P 2018, *Rana,* Soul Light Publishing

Williamson, P 2018, *Earth Warrior*, Animal Dreaming Publishing

Williamson, P 2020, *The Division: The Split in Humanity*, Animal Dreaming Publishing

* Sadly, Capall Bann Publishing was dissolved as a company in early 2021. Paul's books from there are no longer available. However, Paul intends to reprint these books with new editions soon.

FURTHER RECOMMENDED READING

Newton, M 1994, *Journey of Souls*, Llewellyn Worldwide Publications, Woodbury.

Newton, M 2000, *Destiny of Souls,* Newton, Michael, USA.

Woolger, R 1988, *Other Lives, Other Selves,* Bantam, New York.

Weiss, B 1988, *Many Lives, Many Masters,* Touchstone, New York.

NOTES

NOTES

NOTES

NOTES

NOTES

NOTES

NOTES